Crossings

Crossings

Beginnings and Endings in the Regent College Chapel
1988-2000

Walter C. Wright, Jr.

REGENT COLLEGE PUBLISHING
Vancouver

Published 2001 by Regent College Publishing,
an imprint of the Regent College Bookstore,
5800 University Boulevard, Vancouver, B.C. Canada V6T 2E4
www.regentpublishing.com

Chapter 22 ("Leadership and Power") was first delivered in
the Regent Chapel. It was subsequently expanded and published
as the first chapter of Walter C. Wright, *Relational Leadership:
A Biblical Model for Leadership Service* (Paternoster, 2000).

Views expressed in works published by Regent College Publishing are those of
the author and do not necessarily represent the official position of Regent College.

On the cover: Banners by Mae Runions in the Regent College Chapel.
Left to right: Creation, Incarnation, Crucifixion & Resurrection, Pentecost,
Second Coming of Christ.

Unless otherwise noted, Scripture taken from the Holy Bible,
New International Version © 1973, 1978, 1984 by International Bible Society.
First published in Great Britain 1979. Used by permission of Hodder & Stoughton,
a member of Hodder Headline Group. All rights reserved.
"NIV" is a trademark of International Bible Society. UK trademark number 1448790.

Canadian Cataloguing in Publication Data

Wright, Walter C.
Crossings

ISBN 1-57383-190-5

1. Regent College—History. 2. Theology—Study and teaching
(Higher)—British Columbia—Vancouver—History. I. Title.

BV4160.R44W74 2001   230'.071'171133   C00-911031-3

To Beverly
my beta tester

Contents

Chapter	Page
Crossing the River (Joshua 1:1-9)	11
The Theological Education of Isaac (Hebrews 11:1-3, 8-20)	21
Thriving in Exile: A Well-watered Garden (Jeremiah 32:6-15; 31:10-14)	29
The Wisdom of the Sherpas (Psalms 23)	39
The Paraplegic (Luke 5:17-26)	47
Into the Wilderness (Psalm 73; Matthew 4:1-11)	53
Theological Education at a Desert Well (John 4:1-26)	63
Leaving Bethel (Genesis 28:10-22)	71
Encountering Jesus (Mark 10:32-45)	79
Launching a New Adventure (Jeremiah 29:1-14)	87
Who am I? (Exodus 3:1-15)	95
So Now Go and bring my people out (Exodus 4:1-20)	103
Great Expectations (John 13:1-30)	111
Living Proof (John 12:1-11)	119
Coming Together (Philippians 1:1-11)	127
The Last Lecture (Philippians 3:1-4:9)	137
The Character of Community (Colossians 3:1-17)	149
The Character of the Christian in Community (Colossians 1:9-14)	159
Accountability in Community (Philemon)	169
Conflict in Community (Philemon and Colossians)	177
Going Back (Philemon and Colossians)	185
Leadership and Power (Ezekiel 34:1-10, Jude 12-13)	193
Epilogue	203

Introduction

For 12 years I watched God at work in the lives of men and women called from the People of God around the world. Each fall a new community would form in Vancouver as people on a journey with God would gather at Regent College. Every student was a story of God at work — a man or a woman walking with their God — working out the issues of life and vocation in this world. Like salmon drawn upstream, they would leave families, churches, job, even countries — often at great cost — crossing visible and invisible barriers to converge in this city by English Bay.

It was always my privilege to greet the new students and to share with the expanded community in its opening chapel service of worship. The anticipation — the expectation — was palpable. Everyone there was called by God. Everyone was there expecting to meet God and to know him better. The opening chapel of a new year at Regent College was always an exciting event. We would come together before the God who gathered us to worship and celebrate.

And each year I would watch as God did engage his people at Regent. Most years, I would have the new students into my office for lunch or tea in small groups. I would ask them three questions: What has God been doing in your life to bring you to Regent College? What are your expectations for this year at Regent? What do you see as your journey after Regent? We would listen to amazing stories of God at work in individual lives and have the privilege of lifting each other before God in prayer. As the year would unfold, it was normal for us to hear the year described by students as transformational. For many, something died and something was given life — something was broken and something was healed — as God did his work in each life. Those of us on the faculty and staff marveled at the opportunity to walk part of the journey with each new class of students.

Then it was spring. The year was over and graduates would leave, following their God out literally around the world. And again we would gather as a community to worship and celebrate. At the closing chapel it was also my privilege to participate in a service of worship and commissioning. Again, the anticipation — the joy and the sorrow — was palpable. People who had grown to love one another were parting. Friends were leaving friends to scatter widely around the world. Their journey with God was continuing. God was calling. A next step of the journey — often unclear — was opening before them. It was always a service of mixed emotion as we grieved the separation of friends but rejoiced in the new adventure with God before them.

The sermons in this book were part of the opening and closing chapels of Regent College from 1988 to 2000. They were spoken within a community to that community, but they are about a journey that we all are on — a journey of faith — crossing from adventure to adventure in our walk with God. Comings and goings. Beginnings and endings. Crossings of boundaries and borders. May your journey lead you home to the God who walks with you.

—Walter C. Wright, Jr.
Summer 2000

1

Crossing the River

*A*fter the death of Moses the servant of the Lord, the Lord said to Joshua son of Nun, Moses' assistant: "Moses my servant is dead. Now then, you and all these people, get ready to cross the Jordan River into the land I am about to give to them — to the Israelites. I will give you every place where you set your foot, as I promised Moses. Your territory will extend from the desert to Lebanon, and from the great river, the Euphrates — all the Hittite country — to the Great Sea on the west. No one will be able to stand up against you all the days of your life. As I was with Moses, so I will be with you; I will never leave you nor forsake you.

"Be strong and courageous, because you will lead these people to inherit the land I swore to their ancestors to give them. Be strong and very courageous. Be careful to obey all the law my servant Moses gave you; do not turn from it to the right or to the left, that you may be successful wherever you go. Do not let this Book of the Law depart from your mouth; meditate on it day and night, so that you may be careful to do everything written in it. Then you will be *prosperous and successful. Have I not commanded you? Be strong and courageous. Do not be terrified; do not be discouraged, for the Lord your God will be with you wherever you go."*

Joshua 1:1-9

The text we read this morning finds Joshua at the river Jordan. The journey that the Israelites have been taking with God has reached the river. The path goes on, but the river runs through it.

A River runs Through It. In 1992 the Hollywood movie by this name captured the big screen, taking the McLean family's life and offering the river as a metaphor for lines that define and divide us. A river runs through it — in that case a trout stream where a passion for fly-fishing defined the unity of a family. But a river nevertheless that cut boldly through the valley dividing the land and symbolically dividing the family — a family of two brothers — one solid, academic, conservative and religious — the other wild and daring, exciting but unaccountable. The story is told from the perspective of the older brother — Norman — the conservative one, who avoids the risks and survives, while his younger brother — Paul — lives on the edge and eventually pays for it with his life. The river divides the valley and it divides this family. One crossed it . . . but he went alone . . . and died.

The story had poignancy for me in multiple ways. I had a younger brother just like Paul. He was wild and daring and unaccountable, always living in the shadowy margins of what was acceptable. I, of course, am the religious older brother. There was a river of difference between me and my brother. On the week the movie came out — *A River Runs Through It* — my brother was murdered in a knife fight. I saw the movie the day after my brother's funeral. It was powerful — a powerful metaphor of those lines of demarcation, those moments in our lives when we must choose and our future rests on which side of the river we are on.

Watching the movie, however, struck me deeply from another perspective. I have two sons: Damon and Aaron. They could have been cast in the movie. Damon, the older brother is dark and serious and a passionate fly fisherman. Aaron, the younger, is gregarious, relational with curly blond hair just like the Brad Pitt character. The similarities were hauntingly striking. The thought of losing one of them chilling! But if the river runs through my immediate family, it is probably not about lifestyle and risk; it is probably about religion, about faith. My sons understand the Christian story, but so far have not followed Joshua across the river to claim the land that God has for them. That is still my daily prayer.

My brother's funeral was on a Friday, I saw the movie on Saturday. On Sunday morning, Beverly and I were at St. John's for the early morning holy communion — and again I was struck by the common theme. As I knelt at the altar to receive communion, praying for my brother, for myself, and for my sons, I was conscious that I was kneeling before a cross on which another son had died. It was a deeply emotional moment for me as I pondered the Father's loss.

But I also knew that this was why I had hope. Death runs through every life like a defining river, but Jesus has in fact crossed that river and it was a Lord standing very much alive on the other side that I now worshiped. A decision had been made, a river crossed and something new was born.

In my mind that is the kind of imagery that stands behind our text this morning. A river runs through it. A river divides the land and the people. They have come as far as they can go. Now a decision must be made. A river needs to be crossed on this journey they are taking with God. They are being called by God to take the plunge, to accept the risk, to cross the river with the promise that God will go before them and give them the land as he has promised. Another level of trust is being asked for as they are called into the unknown.

And we know the story. The Israelites have been travelling with God through the Sinai wilderness for a few years now since leaving Egypt. They have been following God, learning about his laws and expectations, living in close community, cared for miraculously by God's gracious provision. But these short years of their theological education are now over. It has not been easy, this learning together in such a dependent community, but they have come a long way since the slavery of Egypt. Now their journey brings them to the Jordan. And God wants them to cross over into uncharted territory. The grass may be greener on the other side — flowing with milk and honey — but it's also riskier. So they send out a few representatives to look over the land and bring back a report.

In Numbers 13 we find the account of this exploration: Twelve representatives, one elected from each tribe, are chosen as the advance party to bring back a clear picture of what lies ahead. And they do. They report that the land is as fine as they could ask for. It does indeed flow with milk and honey, fertile for crops and producing wonderful fruit. They bring back huge clusters of fruit to prove their point. It is every bit as good as God promised, even better. But there are a few problems. There are giants out there! The people are strong and hostile. It will not be as easy as it has been here. It might even be quite dangerous.

Ten of the 12 reporters had indeed seen the marvelous land, but their appreciation of its opportunity was overshadowed by the giants they saw. The problems clearly outweighed the possibilities. They recommended strongly that the Israelites just stay where they are and let God take care of them.

Joshua and Caleb, however, saw things differently. They looked with the eyes of wisdom. They saw things from God's perspective. They saw the rich and fertile land and they saw the giants, but they also saw God leading his people and knew that the land was God's. They knew that God would go with them. They called for courage and strength and confidence in the promise that God would go before them.

But the people of Israel listened to the 10. It was too comfortable on this side of the river. In fact the risk of crossing the river seems so great some even proposed undoing all that they had learned these past years and returning to Egypt where at least things were predictable. And we know that they wandered around in the wilderness another 40 years until all those afraid to go across had died. Only Joshua and Caleb remained from the 12 reporters. The Israelites had come to a fork in the road, a river to cross, and had backed away, their lives forever consigned to walking in circles in the desert.

I don't suppose I need to draw out the parallels. We all left another place to be here. We crossed one river to come to Vancouver and invest ourselves in this community. One, two, three, four, or in my case 12 years ago, we started this particular portion of our journey with God. We have learned about God together, we have learned about life from each other, we have cared for one another and we have watched God miraculously take care of this community. It has been a transforming, learning experience. And now, at the end of another academic year, like the Israelites, we stand at the edge of another river. God calls us to cross over, to follow him. He will give us the land and we will serve his people. We have to sort out and act on the reports of those who have been out there.

Neil Postman was here for the Laing Lectures. He talked about information glut in this time of technological revolution. He distinguished between information, wisdom and a narrative foundation for one's action — what I might call faith. Information — wisdom — and faith — three ways to make sense of the world around us. Three ways to look at life after Regent. When I look at the two passages — Numbers 13 and Joshua 1 — I see these three different but related responses emerging as the Israelites faced the river.

First, there is *information*. This is the majority response. The majority were correct. They reported accurate information about the land across the river. There are giants out there! Things will not be easy when we leave the comfort of this community and venture out on this journey with God. There are powerful forces which oppose faith. There are giants who will intimidate us. It's a risky place to go.

This is a world of hunger. Someone dies every 3.6 seconds. It is a world of violence with war in Chechnya and murder in kindergarten. There are disasters in Mozambique and Indonesia. Religious hostility provokes rioting in Nigeria and the Pope has to apologize for the behaviour of Christians. It is a world fueled by greed as dot.com companies make people rich while making nothing of value. Television makes millionaires and marries them off. The majority is correct. There are giants out there. Their knowledge is true, but problems do not tell the whole story.

Caleb knew the problems. He saw the giants. He understood what they were up against. He knew it would not be easy; but he sorted his information with wisdom. He saw things from God's perspective. He trusted God. He believed God and that enabled him to see beyond the giants to a land of milk and honey. He saw marvellous opportunities in this new land. God would protect his people in this land and with that assurance he knew such land would bring blessing. Caleb saw the same things the 10 did. But he looked through the eyes of God and saw what was possible. Where most saw problems, Caleb saw opportunities.

Max DePree likes to talk about the early days of Herman Miller — when his father ran the company. He recalls a time during the depression years when things were difficult for the company. Business was slow; payroll could not be met. At Christmas Max's dad was having dinner at the home of one of the salesmen, Jim Eppinger. It was a memory that stuck in DePree's mind because the home had no Christmas tree and no gifts for the children, and Max's dad knew it was because the company did not have enough money to pay the sales commissions that they owed. The image haunted him long after.

Years later, long after Eppinger had retired as the sales manager who took

Herman Miller through its successful transition into innovative office design, DePree reminisced with Eppinger about that Christmas and how badly he still felt about it. Eppinger looked at him with surprise and commented, "That night was one of the highlights of my life. You couldn't pay my sales commissions, . . . but that night you gave me the New York territory. It was the greatest opportunity I have ever been given." (Adapted from Max DePree, *Leadership is an Art*, Michigan State University Press, 1987, pp. 69-70.)

Like Jim Eppinger, Caleb saw opportunity when everyone else saw problems. He was 40 when he reported things as he saw them (Jos. 14:6-15). And even though he was outvoted, he continued to believe that God would bless his people if they crossed the river. Forty-five years later, as an elder among a new generation of Israelites, Caleb comes back to Joshua still looking through the eyes of wisdom. "So here I am," he says, "eighty-five years old! I am still as strong today as the day Moses sent me out; I'm just as vigorous to go out to battle now as I was then. Now give me this hill country that the Lord promised me that day. You yourself heard then that the giants (Anakites) were there and their cities were large and fortified, but the Lord helping me, I will drive them out just as he said." With Joshua's blessing, Caleb took the land for his inheritance and "the land had rest from war."

Wisdom sees opportunity where information focuses on giants. The perspective of wisdom sees beyond the risks and threats to the possibilities. Caleb believed the promise of God and saw the opportunities that such a land offered.

And finally there is Joshua. As we read in the text this morning, Joshua took God seriously and acted on the promise. He responded in *faith*. He had been one of the 12 who surveyed the land. He knew the same information as the 10. He also knew they were in for some hard times. But like Caleb, he believed God's *promise*. He knew that God would go before him and prepare the land for his arrival. He heard the words of God ringing in his ears: "Be strong and courageous. Do not be terrified; do not be discouraged, for the Lord your God will be with you wherever you go."

Joshua believed and knew that he had to act for the promise to be fulfilled. With this promise, Joshua rallied the people to cross the river and take possession of the land that the Lord their God was giving them for their own. And the story continues.

The problem of information: there are giants out there. The opportunity of wisdom: God will bless his people. And the promise of faith: "Be courageous and go, God is with you."

Information, wisdom and faith. Problems, opportunity and promise. We have them all. Now we too must leave the land on this side where we have felt safe and cross the river into the unknown. It's hard to let go of things we have learned to value, people who have been important to our lives. But like Joshua, we let go and move on so that God can do a new work here and in us.

Sister Macrina Wiederkehr, a Benedictine Oblate, has lived in a variety of monasteries in the course of her ministry. In her little book, *A Tree Full of Angels: Seeing the Holy in the Ordinary*, she writes about "The harvest of good-bye: feasting on the last week at a cherished place." I have found this reflection on leaving and letting go a poignant description of the space in which we find ourselves at the end of an academic year. I read it as a prayer to God. As you think about leaving this community, crossing the river and venturing with God among the giants out there, listen to Sister Macrina:

> It was a wonderful day filled with tears and peace. It all began with my morning prayer. I was praying with the first letter of Peter and was blessed with these words: "Should anyone ask you the reason for this hope of yours, be ever ready to reply . . ." I stopped reading in order to taste my hope more deeply. It is true. A pervading hope that I can't always explain lingers in my soul. And though I am leaving this cherished place where I have lived for four years, the hope will leave with me.
>
> It was a stormy morning. I welcomed it joyfully, because in spite of the hope, I felt a bit stormy inside. It was good of God to dress up the morning to fit my mood. Everyone who lives here is gone today. It is a wonderful gift to my solitude: an empty house, morning, and me. I sat down and brought some of the people I'll be leaving into my prayer: Marietta and Ruben, Paul and Theresa, Joe and Anne Marie, Tami, Janine, Gary and Greg, William, Julie, Catherine, Xavier, Alice, Joe. They filed through my mind and heart into the heart of God. I blessed them and let them go. I ached at letting them go, yet I did it willingly. I leave places well. I think

it has something to do with my pilgrim state and my spirit remembering another land. Still, would it not be treason if I didn't ache a little as I go?...

This afternoon I started packing. I've been throwing things away with a passion. I wish it were as easy to clean up the inside of my life, to throw away my rebellious spirit, my selfishness, my pride and control, my pettiness. The packing continued. I sat down in the midst of my clutter, had a glass of wine, and thought about the Ascension. The Feast of the Ascension is so present to me this year. Unless I go away, the spirit will not come. I do feel that unless I go from here, the spirit cannot do a new thing in my life. And a new thing is wanting to be done. I hear it asking for birth. Who am I to say no to birth?...

I am asking you God, to guard me this week under the shadow of your wings... Keep me from all forms of self-pity. Help me to minister to the end. Keep my hope burning brightly. And should anyone ask me the reason for this hope of mine, I'll be ever ready to explain. It's the life we can't see yet that keeps me ... hoping. It is in our instincts and spirits that something precious is within our reach. (Macrina Wiederkehr, *A Tree Full of Angels*, Harper, 1990, p. 149-150) A new thing is wanting to be born.

Another year is over. It is time to leave a place where we have been fed and nurtured. A river is being crossed, another beginning beckons. Something new will be born in a new place, in a world of overwhelming problems and promising opportunity. It's a new life. It's hard to leave a place where we have been loved, where we have given of ourselves and have grown. It's a risk to cross the river — to start again. But a new thing is wanting to be born and God has promised to go before us.

It is time to leave, time to cross the river. Something new is beckoning. Go out with the knowledge that there will be giants to face, with the wisdom that God will go before you and bless your journey, and with the faith to risk action. Hear the word of God:

"Be strong and courageous, because you will lead the people to inherit the land I swore to their ancestors to give them. Be strong and very courageous. Be careful to obey all the law my servant Moses gave you; do not turn from it to the right or to the left, that you may be successful wherever you go. Do not let this Book of the Law depart from your mouth; meditate on it day and night, so that you may be careful to do everything written in it. Then you will be prosperous and successful. Have I not commanded you? Be strong and courageous. Do not be terrified; do not be discouraged, for the Lord your God will be with you wherever you go."

Joshua 1:6-9

Regent Chapel
April 4, 2000

2

The Theological Education
of Isaac

*N*ow faith is being sure of what we
hope for and certain of what we do
not see. This is what the ancients
were commended for.

*By faith we understand that the universe was formed
at God's command, so that what is seen was not made out
of what was visible. . . .*

*By faith Abraham, when called to go to a place he
would later receive as his inheritance, obeyed and went,
even though he did not know where he was going. By faith
he made his home in the promised land like a stranger in
a foreign country; he lived in tents, as did Isaac and Jacob,
who were heirs with him of the same promise. For he was
looking forward to the city with foundations, whose archi-
tect and builder is God.*

*By faith Abraham, even though he was past age
— and Sarah herself was barren — was enabled to become
a father because he considered him faithful who had made
the promise. And so from this one man, and he as good as
dead, came descendants as numerous as the stars in the sky
and as countless as the sand on the seashore.*

All these people were still living by faith when they

died. They did not receive the things promised; they only saw them and welcomed them from a distance. And they admitted that they were aliens and strangers on earth. People who say such things show that they are looking for a country of their own. If they had been thinking of the country they had left, they would have had opportunity to return. Instead, they were longing for a better country — a heavenly one. Therefore God is not ashamed to be called their God, for he has prepared a city for them.

By faith Abraham, when God tested him, offered Isaac as a sacrifice. He who had received the promises was about to sacrifice his one and only son, even though God had said to him, "It is through Isaac that your offspring will be reckoned." Abraham reasoned that God could raise the dead, and figuratively speaking, he did receive Isaac back from death.

By faith Isaac blessed Jacob and Esau in regard to their future.

Hebrews 11:1-3,8-20

The journey begins . . . God calls . . . You follow . . . prayers are answered, promises are fulfilled . . . and men and women become instruments of God's blessing as the people of God go out around the world. That is what theological education is all about. And, I think, that is what our text is about this morning.

Abraham, father of our faith, patriarch of the people of God. The portion of Hebrews we read this morning is an executive summary of Genesis 12-27, which itself is a short story covering decades in the narrative of Abraham, Sarah, Isaac, Jacob and their relationships with God. It is a story familiar to all of us. It lifts up the call of Abraham — the call to follow God — the beginning of the people of God. Let's find ourselves this morning in this story of God at work.

First, there's Abraham, model for faith, hope and promise — the template for biblical faith — the prototype person of God called out of Ur to follow his God. The father of our faith.

And, of course, there is Abraham the man — husband and father. A man of fear willing to sacrifice his wife to save himself — a father willing to sacrifice his son to follow his God. In Abraham we condemn the former as cowardice and applaud the latter as deep faith. Sometimes unconsciously, I think, the same Abraham who is the model for faith, hope and promise also becomes the model for fear and family pathology as men and women today try to work out what it means to follow their God. Yet in spite of his fear, God blesses him and through him called a people. Theological education calls us to follow God with confidence, in spite of our doubts and fears.

Abraham — a man — called by God. But it's not as simple as that. There are other persons in this story, others who are important to this journey. And each offers a perspective on theological education.

Abraham has heard the call of God. Now he is packing up to leave most of his relatives in Haran to follow God. When I try to imagine this scene two images complete for attention — two pictures clash.

On the one hand, *adventure.* Abraham and Sarah setting off on a trek, a journey with God, a walk of faith, a new beginning in their theological education.

On the other hand, *moving!*

Many of you have just moved to Vancouver. Some of you are still living out of boxes not yet unpacked. You know first hand the other side of this adventure. We have all moved. We know what it is like. Imagine loading everything you own — not even mentioning extended family and your colleagues! — just everything you have accumulated over these years — loading it on the backs of your servants — and whatever beasts of burden Abraham used — packing, walking, setting up home, packing, walking, setting up home. I don't even like to move with a professional moving company! But that is the picture we have here. Everything goes — literally. There is no planned return. And no clear vision about where or when the trek will end. The story is not yet about new locations and settling in, sinking roots. It is about the journey — the walk with God.

Picture it: servants and shepherds running everywhere, packing away the kitchen and dining areas, the quarters for Sarah and her servants — for Abraham, and his contingent — for Lot and his household — the tents, food, clothing and implements of daily living. Shepherds moving the flocks out early getting some distance. Abraham, Sarah and the community following behind as the servants take down the village and pack it up, eager to catch up and pass the travelers so their quarters will be ready when they stop for the night.

As you well know, it may be an act of faith — a journey with God — a trek of a lifetime — but it is still a move!

When we think about Abraham packing up his family, herds and belongings, we must not overlook the servants and shepherds. Abraham walked with God to Canaan. The prototype person of God began a long journey with God — a journey of fear, doubt, hope and faith. But he probably did not carry anything or herd his own flocks. He had servants and shepherds to make his walk with God possible. The story is about a man and a woman on a journey with God. This journey is possible, however, because of the servants and shepherds who cared for them and carried their loads. Hidden men and women hardly recognized in the story. People without status. And yet God blessed their efforts and walked with Abraham.

You pursue your theological education as Abrahams and Sarahs — men and women called by God to faith and hope. But theological education is also about servants and shepherds who carry loads, pitch tents, prepare food, point the direction and help people adjust to the daily journey. If the men and women of this world are going to respond to the call of their God and walk successfully through life as the people of God, they will need servants and shepherds who know the way and are willing to carry their baggage. I think this is also what theological education is all about — preparing a new generation of servants and shepherds to serve the people of God on the journey of faith. Theological education is about service without recognition.

And then there is *Sarah!* There is something about Sarah. Ninety years old and desired by kings. Sarah had a beauty about her that was attractive, that was talked about and acted on. She made an impact on people wherever she went. Called with Abraham, she embarked, willingly we assume, on this endless journey, this continuous move. She too followed her God and pursued his promises.

But if Abraham struggled with fear, and shepherds served without recognition, Sarah wrestled with patience. We don't know how she responded to the daily routine, but I can imagine Beverly's response if each day for years I kept saying, "Not sure where we are going, but we'll go a little further today." Beverly got impatient when I spent 11 years in graduate school and we didn't even have to move! But we do know that Sarah was impatient. She wanted God's promise and when God didn't act fast enough, she brought Hagar into the story to help God along. If God needed help getting on with his promises, Sarah had some ideas. Of course, when Ishmael was born, Sarah became very impatient and jealous and abused Hagar so severely that Hagar and Ishmael had to leave. On a side note here, it always surprises me how easily Abraham goes along with the Hagar plan and then the banishing of Hagar. Maybe he was really afraid of Sarah!

When God does step forward and promise a child, Sarah is 90. Her response is immediate. She laughs out loud. She laughs at God. But God is gracious to Sarah and honors the promise she has been longing for and Isaac is born. Then she laughs for herself. In spite of her impatience, she is used by God to birth the people of God. In God's time, at God's initiative, Sarah becomes the "mother of nations", a partner in the promise, and we hold her up as a model for faith and following. Theological education is about following God's initiative with patience.

And, of course, there is *Isaac*. Have you ever thought about this story from Isaac's perspective? How Isaac must have felt? What Isaac was thinking? What it would be like to be Isaac in this story? We need to think about it from Isaac's perspective because, I think, that is who we are in this story. Isaac, an answer to prayer, a child of promise, a living sacrifice, an instrument of God in spite of himself.

I can imagine Isaac pampered and adored, dark curls bouncing as he toddles around the tent on his chubby little legs. Listening with eyes wide as his doting parents hold him tight and tell him of his birth. It reminds me of a scene we saw once in a campground A mother, a father and the cutest little girl — a bundle of energy and trouble around camp — but a child obviously deeply loved and enjoyed. One evening, seeing her father walking back from the restroom, the little girl stretched out her arms, and toddled out to meet him, calling out, "Me trouble coming!" and was swept up in her father's arms, clearly the joy of his heart. For Beverly and me, that phrase and that embrace have become the epitome of enduring relationship and deep love — "Me trouble coming!" and a welcome embrace — a child generously loved. That's what we have here — a golden child. Isaac is an answer to prayer. How many times did he hear his mother recall her encounter with God, the promise, the laughter, the pregnancy and then Isaac — a gift from God. He is a child of promise. How well did he learn the story of his dad's call, the covenant, the promise of land and the promise that he would be the father of Israel. He was the incarnation of God's promise, deeply loved and probably very spoiled. I imagine that as he grew up he didn't let his parents forget that either. Isaac knew who he was: an answer to prayer, a child of promise, a gift from God, the chosen one, the one through whom God would bless his people.

Then Abraham asked him to go along to worship and sacrifice. I wonder what went through Isaac's mind when he carried the wood up the mountain. "Mount Moriah, a steep hill, heavy load of wood, fire and knife, but nothing to sacrifice. I hope Dad knows what he is doing. We are going to worship the God who declared me the promised child. It needs to be an excellent offering, fitting for my calling, for everything that I am going to do for God."

But when he saw the knife raised to strike and realized that he was the sacrifice, he knew what Abraham and Sarah had learned long ago. "This is not about me. This is about God." Isaac walked down the mountain with a little less swagger, a humble tilt to his head. He had met God; he knew that he was not the promise, only a servant whom God would use. His pride was sacrificed with the ram that God provided. He was an instrument of God's promise, but he was not that promise. The promise was not about him. It was about God. It was about what God was doing in calling a people to be his people. Isaac was just one of the players in the story, like the servants and shepherds.

And just to keep the point before us, the story continues. Isaac goes on with life. He marries the wily Rebekah. He raises two sons and enjoys a good meal of wild game. At the end of his life he prepares to fulfill his role in this story and pass on the blessing to his eldest son Esau. But again, he is reminded — this is not his doing. It is God. The blessing he intends for Esau, God and Rebekah and Jacob conspire to put on the head of Jacob. Jacob is blessed and carries on the promise. Once again Isaac knew, this is God's doing.

A child of promise, an answer to prayer, a living sacrifice, an instrument of God — one player in the story of God's people — just like you and me. Theological education is not about us. It's about God.

It is a new year. A new beginning on your journey with God. Coming to Regent College is like coming to Mt. Moriah — to worship and to sacrifice. Theological education is about your climb to the summit. And your professors have already given you a lot of wood to carry!

You sit here as answers to prayer. Many of you are here today because spouses, parents, grandparents and friends have prayed for you. All of you spent time wrestling with God about the decisions required to pursue theological studies. You are here as the result of the prayer of faculty and staff that God would raise up the men and women who will form the community of Regent College this year. Think about all the people who have prayed for you.

Like Isaac, you are answers to prayer.

You also sit here this morning with your future before you. You are children of God; like Isaac, you are children of promise, bearers of hope. The promise of God will be worked out in your lives and through your lives the people of God will be blessed. Think about those who have invested in you, your education, your growth and health, your coming to Regent. In addition to those you know, I can assure you that a large community of friends supporting Regent College believe that God will bless his people through you. That promise is enough for them to contribute over half of the cost of your theological education. You are children of promise, bearers of hope.

But this is not about you. Theological education is not about you. It is about putting all of your hopes and dreams and expectations and plans for God on the altar. It is about sacrificing your fear, your need for recognition, your impatience and your pride. You come as men and women called by God, but you come also as living sacrifices. You will find yourself on the altar again and again, but you have an advantage over Isaac. You know that the lamb has already been provided. Theological education is not about you. It is about God. Only when you put yourself on the altar as a living sacrifice will you see God at work, around you, in you and through you — in spite of you — as God continues his work and blesses his people.

Answers to prayer. Children of promise. Living sacrifices. Instruments of God. That is our calling. This is our journey.

Regent Chapel
September 13, 1999

3

Thriving in Exile: A Well-watered Garden

*J*eremiah said, "The word of the Lord came to me: Hanamel son of Shallum your uncle is going to come to you and say, 'Buy my field at Anathoth, because as nearest relative it is your right and duty to buy it.'

"Then, just as the Lord had said, my cousin Hanamel came to me in the courtyard of the guard and said, 'Buy my field at Anathoth in the territory of Benjamin. Since it is your right to redeem it and possess it, buy it for yourself.'

"I knew that this was the word of the Lord; so I bought the field at Anathoth from my cousin Hanamel and weighed out for him seventeen shekels of silver. I signed and sealed the deed, had it witnessed, and weighed out the silver on the scales. I took the deed of purchase — the sealed copy containing the terms and conditions, as well as the unsealed copy — and I gave this deed to Baruch son of Neriah, the son of Mahseiah, in the presence of my cousin Hanamel and of the witnesses who had signed the deed and of all the Jews sitting in the courtyard of the guard.

"In their presence I gave Baruch these instructions: 'This is what the Lord Almighty, the God of Israel, says: Take these documents, both the sealed and unsealed copies of the deed of purchase, and put them in a clay jar so *that they will last a long time. For this is what the Lord Almighty, the God of Israel, says: Houses, fields and vineyards will again be bought in this land.*

Jeremiah 32:6-15

"Hear the word of the Lord, O nations; proclaim it in distant coastlands: 'He who scattered Israel will gather them and will watch over his flock like a shepherd.' For the Lord will ransom Jacob and redeem them from the hand of those stronger than they. They will come and shout for joy on the heights of Zion; they will rejoice in the bounty of the Lord — the grain, the new wine and the oil, the young of the flocks and herds. They will be like a well-watered garden, and they will sorrow no more. Then young women will dance and be glad, young men and old as well. I will turn their mourning into gladness; I will give them comfort and joy instead of sorrow. I will satisfy the priests with abundance, and my people will be filled with my bounty," declares the Lord.*

Jeremiah 31:10-14

Good morning, and welcome to another year at Regent College. This week we launch the last full academic year of the twentieth century. It probably sounds a little depressing, but most of you won't complete your studies until the next century! A new year! A new community! I always find it exciting to watch a new year come together at Regent — to watch God form a new community.

It's a small community, a modest piece of land, surrounded by urban diversity. Church, school, library and housing press in on its boundaries, with more housing being developed each year. Economically, it looks like a small unimportant garden — an oasis of community, utilizing space that could be developed into much more profitable enterprise. Cars stream by moving between homes and school, work or church, the busy streets in contrast to the gentle pace of growth in this little community.

It's a diverse community. People come from around the world to see how things are done, to taste the fruit of this community. Everything is interdependent. Each part of the community contributes and each part benefits from the diversity present. As season succeeds season and the year unfolds, the community continually changes, offering a new face to the urban world around it. Things change. Some leave, some stay, some bring new life.

It's an educational community with something to teach the larger frenetic swirl of humanity around its borders — a community seeking to live and model truth that gives definition and purpose to the relationships that make us human. Its impact reaches far beyond its borders. From nearby and from around the world, students and scholars come to study and learn and, in many cases, to find themselves. It is a place of learning and study, of work and enjoyment, of music and art. The publications coming out of this small space have given it a visibility exceeding its size and short history. It has become an international model for growing and educating and nurturing community. It's a garden of life in the midst of urban development, a well-watered garden thriving in exile.

It's called Fairview Gardens and it is located just off highway 101 in Goleta, California. I first learned about Fairview Gardens this summer when I came across a new book by Michael Ableman — *On Good Land: The Autobiography of an Urban Farm.* Michael Ableman came to Fairview Gardens in 1981. It was a small 12 acre organic farm just north of Santa Barbara, less than a mile from the highway. At the time, only a small plot surrounded by large farms, Fairview Gardens was more of a hippy commune than an intentional working farm. But things changed. As Santa Barbara and Goleta grew, the land became more valuable for housing development than for farming. One by one the larger farmers sold out and developers began to design a suburban community. But Michael Ableman refused. He believed deeply that there was a connection between humans and the land that feeds them. He despaired of development that built over the land, and displaced men and women from the processes that produce the food that they eat. He wanted the middle class neighbors who were barbequing in backyards adjacent to the farm to understand their connection to the land that sustains them. He had a vision. He leased the land and developed a self-sustaining organic farm. The book is the story of the struggle between Fairview Gardens and its urban neighbors. It is a story about interdependent relationships and community, about politics and values.

This summer Beverly and I visited the farm. It sits there completely out of place. Twelve acres of green — fruit trees, vegetables, flowers — surrounded by sprawling California ranch-style homes complete with swimming pools — a garden of green jutting up in the middle of a concrete landscape. We walked in the farm with its rows of vegetation shielding it from the houses built right up to its edge. The local library sits at one corner, a church across the street, a school nestles along one side. The rest is houses and busy streets.

Over time the relationship between the farm and the neighborhood has healed because of the patient vision of its founder, Michael Ableman. From antagonism the relationship has moved to cooperation. Fairview Gardens has become a place where schools bring their children to learn about the land, about food, about growing, about themselves. The farm has become part of the community, the provider of fruit and vegetables for the residents of the neighborhood. Crops change with the seasons. They are picked ripe and sold at a street stand on one corner of the farm. Neighbors know that they will pay a little more, but that the peach they buy was probably picked that morning, ripe and ready to eat. The farm has become both an educational center and a community center. People do come from around the world to study its processes or to intern in its fields. The old farm house where the Ablemans live is used for summer concerts and educational workshops. So successful has Fairview Gardens been in its vision to stand for land and good food and community in the midst of urban development that it is now owned by the community. When the owner of the land finally decided to sell to the developers, Ableman pulled together a cooperative of neighbors who had learned to value the vision of this obstinate farmer who kept putting manure on trees near their backyards. One hundred twenty-five families bought a "share" in the produce of the farm. Each Thursday morning they drive in for the bags of lettuce, carrots, beets, turnips, avocados, — whatever is ripe that week. From this initial cooperative effort emerged the Center for Urban Agriculture, a non-profit enterprise, with its board of directors that now run the farm.

Fairview Gardens continues to thrive — a small plot of land, a small community of people who believe in the process of life and the relationship between people and the land that sustains them. As Ableman says, the planting of a tree is an act of faith, the existence of the farm is a statement of his deep beliefs, and Fairview Gardens exists today as a model for community gardens in an urban world.

When I first heard of Fairview Gardens I thought of two things: First, the obvious parallels to Regent College that were evident in my description of the farm. And second, the passage we read this morning from Jeremiah. For Jeremiah, as for Michael Ableman, a small piece of land represents truth and hope in the midst of complexity and brokenness. Jeremiah, prophet of gloom, calls the people of God to repent, and forecasts their defeat and exile. But he does more. He holds out the promise of God to recreate his people, to replant them in the land, to redeem them and be their shepherd. The people of God will once again bloom like a well-watered garden filled with the bounty of the Lord.

And in beautiful prophetic symbolism, Jeremiah buys a piece of land in his hometown, knowing full well that the country will be overrun and the people dispersed into exile. He believes God. He knows also that the people of God will return. They will be restored to their land, redeemed by their God. The purchase of land is an act of faith, a message of confidence in the promise of God, a sign of hope in a time of despair. One piece of land in one of a nation under siege from within and without — a witness to the promise that God will restore his people.

And that is what I think we are about when we gather like this for another year, when we come together from around the world to form a new community in one corner of a major university, in one corner of an urban center, in one corner of Canada. Regent College was founded 30 years ago and exists today as an act of faith, a statement of faith and a model of faith.

Why did you come to Regent? I have seen your application profiles. You come for a variety of reasons, with a mix of expectations. Some of you come for grounding in your faith, for foundational knowledge in bible and theology. Some of you come to think through the integration of your faith with the work to which God has called you. That's why we have such great diversity in our student body. Some of you are here to prepare for leadership in the church, to understand the role and the shape of the church in the next century. And you are here to meet God — to spend time before God in the presence of a challenging and nurturing community.

You have come to Regent College with multiple expectations, with diverse agendas. But your coming to Regent was an act of faith. Like Jeremiah you are making a personal investment in the kingdom of God — an act of hope that the reign of God will ultimately define the whole world. Every hour you invest in your studies, every relationship to which you give your energy is an act of worship, an acknowledgment that God's relationship to his people is defined by their gathering around and following Jesus. We come together this year, we gather this morning because we know that God is here and that Jesus will return again to form a universal Regent-like community (without tuition and exams). This year is an act of worship, an act of hope, an act of faith.

But why do we persist in bringing you all to Vancouver in the day of the Internet? This is a question that will be asked increasingly as technology changes the way we learn, as the world-wide web and sophisticated educational software bring information and interaction into our living rooms. But gathering in community is central to who we are. It is part of what we teach. It is, in fact, how we teach.

As a Christian community, how we live is as important as what we say — maybe more important. How faculty live their lives each day, how we manage our time and our relationships teaches more about theology than our lectures. How students live their lives each day teaches more about what you are learning than the exams you sit. How we live our lives together as organization and community teaches the outside world as much about God as our preaching, writing and evangelism because our behavior always reflects what we really believe.

Regent College is more than teaching and learning. It is teaching and learning and worshiping in community. It is living as community — because Regent College is also a statement of faith, a proclamation to the world that there is in fact a kingdom of God.

In preparation for the fall faculty retreat, Gordon Fee has us all reading the book *Missional Church*. In this study Darrell Guder and his research team explore the nature of the church in the twenty-first century and emphasize its existence as an alternative culture — a visible statement that the kingdom of God is now — that the reign of God has already begun. Regent College, as one expression of the church, the body of Christ, stands as a preview of the kingdom. Sitting in this room is a community of people representing over 30 different nationalities, but a community of people holding dual citizenship in one kingdom. The very existence of Regent on the UBC campus is a statement of faith in the promise of God. Like the church, indeed for the church, we exist as a proclamation of the reign of God, a taste of redeemed humanity, a garden growing in a secular urban city.

And that means *we are a model of faith*. We sit here on the edge of the university to offer a visible example, a sample taste, a fragrant aroma. How we live this year together is an important part of our calling, of our mission. We are a model of faith — in everything that we do. And sometimes that concerns me. The church has not always modeled well. Do we?

I spent much of my summer in the company of good people — but good people who do not recognize the kingdom of God — good people who do not accept the Lordship of Jesus — good people who enjoy and care for one another — who manifest many of the fruit of the spirit in their daily lives and work — people who accept a concept of God — perhaps even one that compels them to do good for others — but little concept of sin, accountability, the redemption of Christ or the forgiveness of God. What distresses me is that they see nothing in the church that convinces them of an alternative culture — a kingdom of God. They see religion as the cause of wars, Christianity as narrow, exclusive and divided within. They see churches as anachronistic, holding on to past traditions, not demonstrating the new reign of God. Now, I know that churches do provide for many Christians a living expression of the alternative culture, but I am concerned that so many people out there cannot see the church as a preview of the reign of God — or worse, they do see it as a preview and decide to pass. Are we any better?

Are we the church? Not really. With all of our diversity we are too homogeneous to truly represent the Body of Christ. We are more like a gathering of brains and ears and mouths! — lacking much of the enrichment of the rest of the body. But we are part of the Body and we seek to live the alternative culture of the kingdom. We are under the Lordship of Christ. And what we learn together about living as a preview of the kingdom, a model of faith, can contribute to the shape and health of the church as we go out from here into communities of faith around the world. Perhaps we should see ourselves as a laboratory for the church — a place where the skills of living together as a model of faith can be practiced and sharpened for the real life of living after Regent.

We do not have time this morning to reflect much on the character of our life together. But we will be doing that all year. However, when I think about the aroma of community, I always to turn Colossians 3. This was the passage that I used for the meditation at my son's wedding, and on which I wrote Aaron and Monique a long letter about the character of marriage that they read at each anniversary. (At least they tell me that they do!) This is what I hope people see when they look at us this year:

> Therefore, as God's chosen people, holy and dearly
> loved, clothe yourselves with compassion, kindness,
> humility, gentleness and patience. Bear with each other
> and forgive whatever grievances you may have against

one another. Forgive as the Lord forgave you. And over all these virtues put on love, which binds them all together in perfect unity. Let the peace of Christ rule in your hearts, since as members of one body you were called to peace. And be thankful. Let the word of Christ dwell in you richly as you teach and admonish one another with all wisdom, and as you sing psalms, hymns and spiritual songs with gratitude in your hearts to God. And whatever you do, whether in word or deed, do it all in the name of the Lord Jesus, giving thanks to God the father through him.

Colossians 3:12-17

Several years ago, based on this passage, I drafted a statement of the character of the College as an organization with a mission *and* a community of the kingdom. It hangs in my office as a reminder to me of the life to which this community has been called, a model of faith to which I am prepared to be held accountable.

A new year begins at Regent. A new community is forming. We are here to learn, but we are also here as a garden planted by God, a preview of the kingdom of God, a model of life in the Body of Christ.

This summer Beverly and I spent the weekend with our son Aaron and his wife Monique, visiting the new home they are renting in California. The day before we arrived Aaron and Monique decided to do a little gardening. Just outside the door leading from their kitchen into their backyard, a large flowering plant was dominating the landscape. Monique did not like the way the plant looked or smelled, so they decided to prune it back a little. Aaron got the hedge clippers. He trimmed back one side — but too much. So he trimmed back the other side — also too much. Back and forth he cut never quite matching his action with the intention of Monique's instructions. Finally, in frustration he grabbed the plant and yanked it out of the ground, roots and all, and then had to cut it up into small enough pieces to fit in the trash bags that they had to go out and buy following this small pruning assignment.

When we arrived, the land beside the kitchen door was quite barren and desolate. But Aaron was already composing a strategy for his confession to the landlady whose plant he had just eradicated, and Monique was preparing to plant a Mexican sage. Now it is a scarred patch of empty earth, but they have faith that by spring, it will be filled with a lush garden of herbs, whose fragrant aromas will seep through their kitchen.

This year we plant a new garden at Regent College. We do not plant in desolate ground. We plant in fertile soil — a community of the people of God that God has been cultivating for 30 years. You are the garden. You are the herbs and peaches and corn and apples and pomegranates. We will live and study together in interdependent diversity.

May the aroma of this garden be a sweet aroma to God and a fragrant attraction in the City of Vancouver. May we together be an act of faith, a statement of faith and a model of faith in this world.

Regent Chapel
September 15, 1998

4

The Wisdom of the Sherpas

*T*he Lord is my shepherd, I shall not be in want. He makes me lie down in green pastures, he leads me beside quiet waters, he restores my soul.

He guides me in paths of righteousness for his name's sake.

Even though I walk through the valley of the shadow of death, I will fear no evil, for you are with me; your rod and your staff, they comfort me.

You prepare a table before me in the presence of my enemies.

You anoint my head with oil; my cup overflows.

Surely goodness and love will follow me all the days of my life, and I will dwell in the house of the Lord for ever.

Psalm 23

On October 15, 1978, Irene Miller and Vera Komarkova, with two Sherpas, stepped onto the summit of Annapurna, 26,545 feet high in the Himalayan mountains of Nepal. It was a moment of celebration. For months these two women, along with eight colleagues under the leadership of Arlene Blum, had planned and advanced the necessary stages to place a climbing team on Annapurna's peak. Blum's expedition was the first American expedition to climb Annapurna and the first team of all women climbers to ascend one of the world's 8000-metre mountains. With the help of their Sherpa guides, the expedition had succeeded.

Arlene Blum was monitoring things from camp three — and she was excited! It had been hard, but her dream was finally accomplished. As the expedition had moved up the mountain, the altitude and weather had taken their toll. Only four climbers still had the strength to even think about climbing beyond camp four. But the first team had made it. Miller and Komarkova with their two guides had reached the summit. Blum contacted the second team at camp four and gave them the news. Good News! The expedition was a success! The Sherpas advised against a second team attempt, so Blum called everyone down from the mountain with thanks and celebration.

For the two women waiting at camp four, Alison Chadwick and Vera Wilson, however, this was not good news. While they celebrated the success of the expedition, it was not enough to be part of the team that had put two women on top of Annapurna. They each wanted to be one of the women who reached the summit. And that personal objective clouded their judgement. Ignoring the advice of the Sherpas, they decided to try for a secondary summit on the side of Annapurna — one that had never been climbed. They roped up and headed for camp five without their guides. They never made it. Somewhere below the high camp they lost their footing and fell to their death. Another successful expedition marred forever by tragedy. They should have listened to their Sherpas.

Many of you know that I have been on sabbatical leave part of this year and that for my vacation I spent the month of November in Nepal, participating in a trek to the Base Camp of Mount Everest and the relatively small Khumbu peak of Kala Pattar. Now the only points of connection between my trek and Blum's expedition are that they were both in Nepal and both were dependent upon Sherpas — beyond that it was different leagues! But it's the Sherpas I want to talk about. These gentle people, living high in the Himalayas, are known for their remarkable endurance, their expertise as guides and the amount of oxygen their blood carries. While we normal mortals are gasping for oxygen in the thin air, the Sherpas are carrying their weight or more in baskets hanging from their heads. They are amazing. Sherpas are also very wise about matters of mountain climbing and daily living.

On our trek we had three Sherpa guides: Jamyang, Santosh, and Suresh. I grew to appreciate them greatly over our time together. They gave us important advice and modeled it as we walked the mountains together. There are three lessons I learned from the Sherpas that I would like to share with you as you finish the year at Regent and move out on your own trek, your own journey from here with God. Three lessons the Sherpas underlined at the beginning and modeled throughout the trip:

1. Walk your own pace.

2. It's the journey that matters, not how high or how far you can go.

3. The people you serve are more important than the summits you climb. Three truths about trekking — three lessons for life.

Walk your own pace

Long before the trek even began, this was the mantra repeated over and over by the guides: "Walk your own pace. You do not have to keep up with anyone. You don't have to be Edmund Hillary or Arlene Blum. Be yourself. Walk the pace that is comfortable for you. If you push yourself faster than your pace, you will waste your strength. But similarly, if you walk slower than your pace, you will also burn off your energy. You have nothing to prove by how fast you go. Be yourself — and walk your own pace!" Wise advice, with application far beyond a mere trek in the mountains.

We heard this advice from the Sherpas every day as they encouraged us up the mountain trail. And they reinforced it with their leadership. As we climbed into the Himalayas, one of the guides would go in front leading the way, keeping a pace always a little faster than the fastest trekker. This way he was always in place to point the direction, to make sure the trail was safe, to keep anyone from wandering off on a wrong path and to prepare for our next stop. At the same time, a second Sherpa always came behind, following the group, watching for stragglers, encouraging the slower walkers and making sure that everyone, even the slowest, felt like part of the group. An appropriate pace was anywhere between the lead Sherpa and the following Sherpa — and you could not walk faster than the lead guide nor slower than the following one. The third Sherpa walked with us, talking and encouraging everyone as we moved at our own pace, pointing out sights and animals, naming the mountains and villages, monitoring the condition of the trekkers, working to see that we got the most out of our daily experience. No matter where you were on the trail, you always were part of the group, you were always included and encouraged. You always belonged. You were surrounded by leadership.

It is hard for me to reflect on this three-part model of leadership — going before, going with and following behind — without thinking of the psalm we heard this morning. Derek Kidner articulated this three-part outline of God's shepherding leadership in a Regent chapel several years ago. The well-known 23rd Psalm falls into three parts with the Shepherd God first, leading his people along the path that he chooses to lush meadows and restful lakes and rivers, then walking with his people through the ups and downs of life with comfort, encouragement and kingly protection, and finally personified as goodness and love, following his people until they are safely home in his presence.

That is what the Sherpas modeled in their leadership. They went before us, walked with us and followed up behind to ensure that each one of us could walk at our own pace. They led us — just like God does.

I think this Sherpa advice is important as you finish this year and move out to continue your journey with God. Walk your own pace. It's not too fast or too slow for God. You have nothing to prove; be yourself. It's the only person you can be. And trust your guide. You do not take this journey alone. God has already gone on ahead to prepare the trail. He will be with you in the good times and the bad times, and he will not let you fall behind. In fact, there is no behind. There is only the next step — and God takes that with you. As you leave Regent, walk your own pace and enjoy your journey with God.

It's the journey that matters, not how high or how far you can go

This second piece of advice was repeated almost as much as the first one. From the first day, the Sherpas told us not to focus on the summit as the measure of success. They told us that a third of the trekkers in most groups cannot acclimatize to the elevation in the limited time that we had available. A third of us would not reach the summit. And consistently the Sherpas refused to talk about distance. Never would any guide refer to miles or kilometers. It was always days. Partly this is due to the impact that altitude and elevation have in measuring distance. It takes 10 days to walk from Lukla to Lobuche. But it takes four days to walk from Lobuche to Lukla. But partly they didn't focus on distance because they were not measuring by destination. They focused on one day at a time. They encouraged us to come for the trek not the summit. The summit of Kala Pattar above the Everest Base Camp is only one point on the trek — and not everyone going their own pace should expect to go there. If the destination becomes the measure of success, many factors — health, weather, altitude — could made the trek a failure. If the trek is the destination, the trip will be a success regardless of how far we go.

I knew this advice. I know it as someone who has been turned back from several mountain summits because of weather or health or skill. And basically, I have lived most of my life with this philosophy. I really do believe that life is about living — not accomplishments! But on this trip I was little better than the second team on Blum's Annapurna climb. I had flown halfway around the world to participate in this trek. But I came for the wrong reason. I wanted to go to the Khumbu basin, to climb higher than 18,000 feet and look down on the Everest Base Camp. And I figured that I might not have such an opportunity again. So I focused strongly on the destination and channeled my energy each day to eating, drinking, sleeping and staying healthy enough for the next day's trek. Without even realizing it, I walked past incredibly beautiful sights focused on staying healthy enough for tomorrow. At 14,000 we were snowed in for three days and faced the high probability that we might not be able to go higher because of deep snow and no visibility. If you read my journal for those nights, you can see me trying to justify why the trip was a success even if we turned around there. It's not very convincing.

When I look at my pictures now, I am surprised how beautiful it was where we were snowed in at Dingboche. Yet in my journal for those days I am complaining about the snow, the altitude and the pungent smell of burning yak dung!

I would like to tell you that God met me at 14,000 feet; that I recognized the error of my ways, saw the beauty of the past two weeks, and went on not needing to reach the summit. Unfortunately that is not what happened. I had a very difficult time communicating with God on this trek, and I did not let go of the summit until I had reached it. Only on the way down did I begin to realize that this was an incredibly beautiful country we were passing, with remarkable villages and wonderful people. Only on the way down did I stop worrying about my health and strength and find time to reflect with God on what was happening. And then I got depressed. Then I realized that this goal that I have had for years — this trek to the Mt. Everest Base Camp — was behind me. It was over. The adventure of my life was done. That is a depressing thought!

It took me several days back home before I regained perspective and realized what I had done. I had focused on a destination at the expense of the journey. And like all destinations, when I got there I found it was only one more point on the journey — not the end. My need to reach the summit, teamed with my uncertainty about my ability to make it, focused all of my energy on tomorrow to the extent that I did not enjoy being with God today. So I think I'll just have to go back and do it again — the right way! Which also means that I realize the journey continues, and God knows what adventures still lie ahead!

As you leave this community and venture forth with God, try to remember the advice of the Sherpas. "It is the journey that matters, not how high or how far you can go." For some of you, coming to Regent has been like climbing a mountain. Leaving the rarified air of academia will make your breathing easier, but it might also leave you a bit depressed if it has been an intense experience this past year. But Regent is just one high point on a continuing trek. The God with whom you studied here is the one who walks down the trail with you.

Don't let the pursuit of objectives distract you from the journey at hand. Live each day one at a time. It's a trek, not a climb. There is no end point to shape your days — only the daily relationship with God. It does not matter what you accomplish or where you go. What matters is who you walk with. Your trek is about living. Don't get distracted by summits. Your destination is God — the one who goes before you, walks with you and follows behind, keeping his people together.

The third lesson that I draw from the Sherpas comes more from observing their action rather than hearing their advice. And yet it is the obvious corollary to focusing on the journey.

The people you serve are more important than the summits you climb

Suresh was the youngest Sherpa. He is a first year business student at the University in Kathmandu. He had been on many treks before as porter and apprentice, but this was his first trek as a guide. He was the assistant Sirdar, the assistant guide and manager of the porters. He watched over us with great care as Jamyang and Santosh watched over him. He took his turn leading, walking with us and following behind, always smiling, always encouraging. It was clear to all of us that the Sherpas were there to serve us. They were more interested in guiding us safely along the trail than achieving the summit. They wanted us to enjoy each day in their country whether or not we reached the

Base Camp. Suresh's warm smile and ready wit made him a welcome companion along the trail. I would have liked to have shared the excitement of reaching the summit with Suresh. But Suresh did not make it to the summit of Kala Pattar. He did not get to the Khumbu valley on this trek. When one of the trekkers, Kristina, became ill at 16,000 feet, Suresh stayed behind and escorted her down to the nearest hospital, seeing that she was cared for until we descended. The summit was not important; Kristina was. And to this day, Kristina thinks that Suresh was the best guide on our trek. He was there to assist us on our journey, whether it meant helping someone up a steep portion of trail or helping Kristina down to the hospital. Suresh, like all of our guides, understood that serving the people with whom he walked was more important than the summits he climbed. The Sherpas were there to walk with us and help us get the most out of each day's trek.

Again, I think there is wisdom here for us. We go out from here on a journey with God. But we are not alone on the trail. The path is filled with trekkers, pilgrims, men and women walking through life seeking to understand the events of each day. You will find other Sherpas on your journey, men and women, who, like those sitting around you this morning, will walk with you for portions of the trip, sharing from their wisdom and experience, ready to help you up rocky places and down slippery slopes.

And they have you to look forward to. You go out from Regent as servants of God, walking with the Shepherd, equipped and ready to serve those placed in your care. You are the Sherpas. You have wisdom and experience to share as you walk with others. Your journey is about service. I believe the final measure of your life will be the people you serve not the summits you climb. Let me say that again: The final measure of your life will be the people you serve not the summits you climb!

We have reached a summit. This is the end of another year. For some of you it is the end of your Regent experience. You have walked together for a year or more. You have cared for one another, learned from one another, laughed with one another and cried with one another. Some of you can see the next adventure beckoning with excitement. Some of you can only see the trail leading away, not quite sure where it goes. But for either group, the Sherpas have another piece of wisdom. When asked what the trail is like from here they laugh, hold up their hand and say, "It's like every Himalayan trail: up and down and up and down and up and down." Wherever you go from here, you can be certain of that. Your journey will go up and down, up and down. And

God knows what's on the other side of the mountain.

So listen to the Sherpas. Be yourself; walk your own pace. That is precisely the pace God is walking. Live for the journey. It's the journey that matters each day, not how high or how far you can go. And serve the people whom God places on your path wherever it leads.

Go out with God, confident in the promise that your Shepherd has gone before you, will walk with you and surrounds you completely as he leads you home.

Regent Chapel
April 20, 1999

5

The Paraplegic

*O*ne day as he was teaching, Pharisees and teachers of the law, who had come from every village of Galilee and from Judea and Jerusalem, were sitting there. And the power of the Lord was present for him to heal the sick. Some people came carrying a paralytic on a mat and tried to take him into the house to lay him before Jesus. When they could not find a way to do this because of the crowd, they went up on the roof and lowered him on his mat through the tiles into the middle of the crowd, right in front of Jesus.

When Jesus saw their faith, he said, "Friend, your sins are forgiven."

The Pharisees and the teachers of the law began thinking to themselves, "Who is this fellow who speaks blasphemy? Who can forgive sins but God alone?"

Jesus knew what they were thinking and asked, "Why are you thinking these things in your hearts? Which is easier: to say, 'Your sins are forgiven,' or to say, 'Get up and walk'? But that you may know that the Son of Man has authority on earth to forgive sins. . . ." He said to the paralysed man, "I tell you, get up, take your mat and go home."

Immediately he stood up in front of them, took what he had been lying on and went home praising god. Everyone was amazed and gave praise to God. They were filled with awe and said, "We have seen remarkable things today."

Luke 5:17-26

Well here we are. It's September already. Another year begins! I like September. It's kind of like the academic equivalent of spring — new students sprouting all around — perennial students returning for another year seasoned by the summer sun — and a few evergreens who studied at Regent straight through summer school. It's a time of blossoming enthusiasm — new life and energy — new hopes and expectations.

I have been a little more aware of seasonal cycles since I read a marvelous little book this summer entitled *Epitaph for a Peach*. David Masumoto, a California fruit farmer, writes almost poetically about his relationship with the land and his expectations for a delicious variety of peach. David grows Sun Crest peaches. Sun Crest peaches are organically grown, rich with texture, dripping with juice and exploding with taste. He has great expectations for this peach. He is carefully cultivating it for the gourmet food market. But there is a problem. As a piece of fruit, it exceeds his highest expectations. But as a marketable commodity, his Sun Crest peaches fall short. They turn an amber gold color instead of the deep red that people associate with ripe peaches, and they need to be eaten soon after they are picked. They taste wonderful but have too short a shelf life for fruit brokers and markets. In the end, as the farmers review their year, David realizes that in spite of his patient effort, he has to adjust his expectations for his delicious peach. The gourmet specialty food market did not buy his peaches. Rather, he sold them to a baby food company. Instead of forming the centerpiece of exclusive fruit baskets, his Sun Crest peaches were pureed and bottled for babies. This was not what he expected, but it keeps his peach alive and offers hope for another year. His little book was written as an epitaph for the Sun Crest peach, but it is more. It is a story of life and the redirected hope of altered expectations.

The passage from Luke is woven with the threads of expectation. A gathering of high expectation — not unlike an opening chapel at Regent. People crowded in, standing room only — bringing their lives before Jesus, expecting to learn and to be healed. Religious leaders hovering like theological educators

— professionally trained to teach and heal and monitor the learning process.

Jesus is there in the center teaching and healing people, surrounded by Pharisees and religious scholars from all over Galilee and Judea. Everyone is crowding around with expectation, wanting to be healed or to see this marvelous teaching in action. But the story centers on one person — a paralyzed man with high expectations.

I think it is interesting to put ourselves in the body of this person in the story. What is it like to be permanently crippled? I have my share of aches and pains that come with an aging body, but I have never broken a bone, nor experienced any illness that deprived me of the use of my arms and legs. As I child I had a mild case of polio that stiffened my body so that it was not until high school that I could actually touch my toes in exercise. But it was a mild case. It has in no way restricted of my movement. And I can still beat Brent Fearon in racquetball!

In my class, I tell the story of Mark Wellman, the paraplegic who was heralded by the world's press for his successful climb of the El Capitan rockface in Yosemite. A man who stretched beyond his limitations to achieve this feat of skill. And yet, as I point when I tell the story, Mark Wellman could only reach the top of El Capitan because his friend Mike Corbett, roped himself to his crippled buddy, and kept him secure as he worked his way up the 3000-foot wall of rock.

Now Luke is telling us about another paraplegic, a man who wanted freedom from the rigid limitations of his body. He wanted to move again. He wanted to be healed from his crippled condition. And this man also had his own Mike Corbett. In fact he had four friends to help him. We don't know whose idea it was to take the paraplegic to Jesus. Did the crippled man hear of the possibility of healing and draft his four friends to take him to Jesus? Or had his friends seen Jesus in action, healing men and women of various illnesses, and convinced their friend that he must go see Jesus? We don't know how the idea came into their heads, but we do know that the four friends put the crippled man in a blanket, picked up the four corners and took him to the house where Jesus was healing people. But they might as well have been at the foot of El Capitan. They couldn't get in to see Jesus. The building was filled with people wanting to be healed, people wanting to hear the teaching and see this healing happen and some who were skeptical about the whole thing. The place was packed. There was no way they could get in.

Maybe the friends were climbers because they immediately headed for the roof. I imagine that this would have concerned the paraplegic. It's one thing to be carried along level ground in a blanket stretcher held tight by four friends. It's another to be in this blanket when your four friends are climbing unto the roof of a house! I have dangled on climbing ropes completely dependent upon the friends who hold me secure. It takes a high level of trust to let people move you around like this when you are not capable of helping yourself.

They take him up the roof and then they tear up the roof tiles. He might be getting a little concerned by now. Then they must tie ropes unto the four corners of the blanket because they lower him through the roof — right to the feet of Jesus. Now, he must have wanted to be healed very badly or I think he would find this experience rather embarrassing. He can't control his friends; maybe he didn't want to control them. But they tear up the roof, lower him before Jesus and put him at the front of the line of people waiting to be healed. All these people, waiting for who knows how long for the possibility that Jesus might heal them, and suddenly through the roof, the paraplegic cuts in line. His friends put him right at the front. He may well have been embarrassed, but I imagine that any embarrassment would have vanished quickly when he found himself looking into the face of the person who might actually be able to heal him; to free his limbs to able to walk and run again.

Then Jesus looks up at the four faces leaning hopefully over the hole in the roof, responds to their expectant faith and says to the paraplegic, "Friend, your sins are forgiven."

Now if you were the paraplegic how would you feel? You have just endured the humiliation of having your friends pick you up like a bag of potatoes, manhandle you through a hole in the roof and place you at the front of a long line of persons who are also hoping to be healed. But that's okay because you want to be healed. You want to be free from the limitations of a body that can't do what your friends can do. You want to walk. And Jesus says to you, "Your sins are forgiven." How do you feel about that?

We don't really know what the crippled man was thinking because the story in Luke moves immediately to the exchange between Jesus and the religious leaders, who see these words for what they are: a claim to be God. But what do you think the paraplegic is thinking about now?

I bet he has forgotten all about being healed! I can imagine him looking into Jesus' eyes as he speaks and experiences the full reality of God's forgiving love. At that moment he sees himself, not as a crippled man wrapped up in a blanket, but as one who has met Jesus, one who is loved by God, one who has experienced the complete forgiveness of God's love and found his own identity in a wonderful new relationship. He has been healed — in the depth of his soul. That must have been more wonderful than anything he could have imagined. Whether or not he can walk is a secondary issue that pales in comparison. He has a new relationship with God, a new life, because of this encounter with Jesus. That is more than enough.

Perhaps for our benefit the story should have stopped here so its point would be more poignant. It is not a story about healing. It is an encounter with God. It is about an experience of the forgiving love of God, present in the life, ministry and death of Jesus. It is about a new immediate relationship with God present in Jesus.

But Luke goes on. After the theological debates are out of the way, Jesus does return to the paraplegic and heals him, interestingly, by telling him to do exactly what he wanted to be able to do — get up, pick up his blanket and walk out of there. Jesus doesn't tell him he is healed. Basically, he just says, "Go on, get out of here." And he does. He went home and told everyone he saw about God. Luke concludes this story with the point he wants to make. The paraplegic does not go home telling people about Jesus healing him. He goes home praising God! This is a story about an encounter with God, in Jesus, that transforms a life forever The physical healing I believe is secondary. It is a story about relationships: a story of a man and his friends; a man with Jesus; Jesus and God; and, therefore, a story of a man in relationship to God.

We come to this new academic year with a variety of needs. We have come to learn. We have things that we need God to take care of. We have wounds that need healing. We bring questions and concerns about our life, our living as members of this community. We have worries about housing, money, family, time. We bring these to God. We seek the healing touch of Jesus.

But what Luke promises us is not necessarily the desired solution to our problems. He offers us the healing of our souls. An encounter with God, an experience of God's loving forgiveness, in which we will find ourselves and renew our relationship with God through Jesus Christ. That is what theological education is all about. That is what this year we will spend together is all about.

When we place a graduate school of Christian studies — this community of Regent College — alongside of the picture that Luke offers us of a crowded room gathered around Jesus, we realize that there are two sets of roles in Luke's story in which we can see ourselves. Students crowding into the classrooms, overflowing the chapel can easily identify with the people pressing to get close enough to see and hear Jesus. Those of us on the faculty and staff can easily fall into the roles of religious leader and teacher and critic. But that's the wrong picture.

As we enter this new year as a community of learning and worship, may God grant you the role of the paraplegic in all its vulnerability and dependence, and allow you to experience the healing of his forgiving love in the presence of Jesus. And I pray that the faculty and staff might find themselves on the roof, tearing up tiles and cutting holes in our shelter and security, doing whatever it takes to place you at the feet of Jesus. You may find healing or truth or wisdom this year; but we want you to bask in the presence of Jesus — in the power of God's forgiving love.

And when this year is over, may we all hear the words of Jesus: "Friend, your sins are forgiven; get up, take your things, and go on home living your life in the praise of God."

Regent Chapel
September 9, 1997

6

Into the Wilderness

Surely God is good to Israel,
* to those who are pure in heart.*
But as for me, my feet had almost slipped;
* I had nearly lost my foothold.*
For I envied the arrogant
* when I saw the prosperity of the wicked.*

They have no struggles;
* their bodies are healthy and strong.*
They are free from common human burdens;
* they are not plagued by human ills.*
Therefore pride is their necklace;
* they clothe themselves with violence.*
From their callous hearts comes iniquity;
* the evil conceits of their minds know no limits.*
They scoff, and speak with malice;
* in their arrogance they threaten oppression.*
Their mouths lay claim to heaven,
* and their tongues take possession of the earth.*
Therefore their people turn to them
* and drink up waters in abundance.*
They say, "How can God know?

Does the Most High have knowledge?
This is what the wicked are like —
  always carefree, they increase in wealth.
Surely in vain have I kept my heart pure;
  in vain have I washed my hands in innocence.
All day long I have been plagued;
  I have been punished every morning.

If I had said, "I will speak thus,"
  I would have betrayed your children.
When I tried to understand all this,
  it was oppressive to me
  till I entered the sanctuary of God;
  then I understood their final destiny.

Surely you place them on slippery ground;
  you cast them down to ruin.
How suddenly are they destroyed,
  completely swept away by terrors!
As a dream when one awakes,
  so when you arise, O Lord,
  you will despise them as fantasies.

When my heart was grieved
  and my spirit embittered,
  I was senseless and ignorant;
  I was a brute beast before you.

Yet I am always with you;
  you hold me by my right hand.
You guide me with your counsel,
  and afterward you will take me into glory.
Whom have I in heaven but you?
And earth has nothing I desire besides you.
My flesh and my heart may fail,
  but God is the strength of my heart
  and my portion forever.

Those who are far from you will perish;
  you destroy all who are unfaithful to you.

But as for me, it is good to be near God.
  I have made the Sovereign Lord my refuge;
  I will tell of all your deeds.

Psalm 73

  Then Jesus was led by the Spirit into the desert to be tempted by the devil. After fasting forty days and forty nights, he was hungry. The tempter came to him and said, "If you are the Son of God, tell these stones to become bread."

  Jesus answered, "It is written: 'People do not live on bread alone, but on every word that comes from the mouth of God.'

  Then the devil took him to the holy city and had him stand on the highest point of the temple. "If you are the Son of God," he said, "throw yourself down. For it is written:
    "'He will command his angels concerning you,
      and they will lift you up in their hands,
        so that you will not strike your foot against a stone.'"

  Jesus answered him, "It is also written: 'Do not put the Lord your God to the test.'"

  Again, the devil took him to a very high mountain and showed him all the kingdoms of the world and their splendor. "All this I will give you," he said, "if you will bow down and worship me."

  Jesus said to him,"Away from me, Satan! For it is written: 'Worship the Lord your God, and serve him only.'"

  Then the devil left him, and angels came and attended him.

Matt 4:1-11

Picture this with me: Five travelers are heading into the desert. Each walks alone, heading to a common destination— a popular place of retreat, a place of silence and solitude but not isolation, a place where men and women go to meet their god, to find themselves, to sort out their lives. Each one is on a spiritual pilgrimage — a personal quest.

Four of them are committed to 40 days of daylight fasting and silence. In the evenings they will gather for meals and conversation, forming a community of sorts, seeking comfort in one another's company. The fifth is pursuing a more rigorous path. His destination will be a little farther out — a little more isolated. He is planning a total fast for 40 days and nights of silence. Five persons on spiritual retreat, each preoccupied with a personal agenda.

Marta, the wife of a wealthy landowner, is childless and running out of time. The law allows her husband to divorce her if no child is born during ten years of marriage. The ten years are nearly up. She enters this retreat seeking a miracle, praying for a baby to sustain her marriage.

Aphas, an elderly brick mason from Jerusalem is dying of cancer. He says he is on retreat to prepare himself for death. But we suspect he too is looking for a miracle, a healing to give his body new life, to give his life new hope.

Shin, part Jew, part Greek, comes from the north — a philosopher of sorts seeking "tranquility." He hides his search for courage and approval behind a stoic posturing.

A badu villager, seemingly crazed but mysteriously comfortable with his desert surroundings.

And Jesus, a young Galilean, communing with his God, seeking the power to heal the hurting people of his world. Five pilgrims heading into solitude.

As they follow the path into the desert wilderness they pass the tent of Musa, an arrogant young trader of fabric and anything else he can get his hands on. Musa has been left behind to die of desert fever, abandoned by his business colleagues. His wife, Mira, late in her first pregnancy, is up in the hills awkwardly digging his grave in the rocky slopes, hoping that Musa will soon fill it. Her life with him has been dominated by physical and emotional abuse.

When Jesus passes the tent he stops for a drink of water. After taking a traveler's portion he bids the unconscious Musa *shalom* — "be well" and continues to his remote desert cave. And with this word, the trader revives, the fever leaves him. And Musa is convinced that Jesus has healed him.

On the basis of this "special miracle," Musa sets himself up as landlord — director of spiritual retreats, and charges his new tenants for the privilege of retreating near his tent. Using his healing and resurrection-like recovery, he extorts everything of value from the four who seek retreat nearby.

With this opening plot, prize-winning novelist Jim Crace launches his new book *Quarantine*, an atheist's look at the temptations of Jesus. The story of seven lives quarantined by choice for 40 days in the Judean wilderness — seven people on a spiritual quest. And in the telling of this story, Crace offers his own subtle temptation: *the quest is not about God; it is about you.* And he says it with such earthy beauty in his words that the book was a finalist for the prestigious 1997 Booker Prize for English novels.

And yet, even in this narrative of desert pilgrimage through the eyes of a skeptic, his primary character believes he was healed — Musa *believes*. And the stories that Musa tells his desert companions are woven with such conviction that the pilgrim Jesus becomes the obsession of each person, the answer to their desperate quests. And led by the arrogant trader with his new lease on life, the pilgrims then become the vehicle of Jesus' temptation as they badger him constantly to leave his desolate cave and come to them — to work his miracles upon them and fulfil their quests.

The author Crace never lets go of his claim that life is about you and me, not about God, even as he is never quite able to shake off the persistent power the fifth pilgrim seems to have in the minds of the others. At the end of the 40 days, Musa, the wily trader, the consummate story-teller, seller of dreams as well as fabrics, returns to his city as a man who has had a spiritual experience, a man who was healed. Does *he* have a story to tell? Maybe even healing to offer? Something to sell? It will make him rich. He has met Jesus. This sets him apart from everyone else. He is important.

As the story ends, though not successful in emptying the Christian narrative of its power, Crace focuses his story on the character of Musa, who will turn his encounter with Jesus into a story about himself. It's about Musa and his spiritual experience. Not about God.

Not your ordinary interpretation of the temptation passage we read this morning! But perhaps this is a commentary worth considering, because Crace's interpretation of the temptation is the temptation offered to us daily by the world around us — to focus on ourselves — to take ourselves too seriously! — "Life is not about God; it's about me." Through the lens of Jim Crace, the temptation to turn stones to bread is the temptation to take ourselves too seriously. The temptation to jump into the arms of angels is the temptation to take our spirituality too seriously. The temptation to worship the devil and win the world becomes the temptation to take our ministry too seriously. In each case it is about taking ourselves too seriously. It's the temptation to take our eyes off of God and focus on ourselves.

When I first read this book I found myself wondering about Regent. This is a place where we come to spend time with God, a place where we retreat for spiritual focus. Is this the wilderness where we face temptation? Is this the desert? But then I remembered how much it rains around here — and I knew this was not the desert!

But then what?

Perhaps with the psalmist, we are simply a sanctuary within the wilderness. A place where we distance ourselves from distractions in order to understand — to gain perspective on what God is in fact doing in this world. The desert, the wilderness, the temptations. That is the world from which we came and into which we return as another year comes to an end.

And the dangerous thing is that your time at Regent might in fact increase your vulnerability to Crace's temptation. The voice of our culture whispers constantly in our ears that life is about me, about you. We know that is not true and we have spent the past year together renewing our focus on God present and at work in our lives and in this world. Yet we have been away on retreat. We have spent time with Jesus. We have concentrated our energy and attention on our walk with God, our spiritual development. The tempta- tion here — one that may actually be hidden in the midst of our corporate desire for growth in faith and spirit — is the temptation to see spirituality as a personal, individual thing. It is easy then to take the next step and believe that life is about me and God. And how much larger will that temptation loom when you leave this community and find yourself hungering for spiritual friendship and godly relationships? How easy it will be to expend all of your energy on your own spiritual formation as a defense against a fast chang- ing world that moves ahead without God. And yet when we step into the sanctuary of God, when we focus our eyes upon God, we see the scope of what he is in fact doing, and we see the people of God of which we are part. Only by lifting our eyes from our own growth to God himself will we see the people of God surrounding us for our mutual encouragement and growth. We are part of something much bigger that God is about.

And then there is the temptation of Musa — the temptation to turn our faith into a business — to become Gnostic in the superior knowledge of a Regent education. We have something special to offer. We have been with Jesus. We are equipped as spiritual leaders, spiritual directors — how easy to offer ourselves as spiritual personal trainers. It is true that we have something wonderful to share, an experience that we wish for all who seek God. But built into the enthusiasm with which we utilize our newly honed exegetical skills and apply our expanded knowledge of God, is the temptation to point to our ourselves — our gifts — the good we can do — rather than to point to God. It is a subtle but profound step when our walk with God declares our godliness . . . rather than God's holiness. How easy it is then to take the next step and think that our representation of God is more important than God's quiet presence with us. And yet again when we step into the sanctuary of God, when we focus our eyes upon God, we see ourselves humbly in perspective as recipients of God's grace. Only by lifting our eyes from our gifts to the God who deploys our giftedness will we see what God is doing and see how we have in fact been used by God. Spirituality is not about our godliness. It is about God.

The third temptation I think is found in our zeal to serve, to make a difference in the world around us. This is the very language that we used when we recruited you to Regent. We want to equip you to make a difference in the world, to influence the lives of the people around you. You go out from this community seriously desiring to serve God, to do kingdom work. And yet I know how easy it is to get ahead of God, to put my own agenda for God ahead of God's agenda for me. In our enthusiasm for the ministry to which God calls us, we can want to do great things for God so badly that we take over the role of God. But again when we step into the sanctuary of God, when we focus our eyes upon God, we regain our perspective. This is not about our ministry, our service. It is not about God blessing our ministry. It is about our faithful recognition that God is actively engaged in the outworking of *his* kingdom — a ministry in which we may be privileged to participate in *his* work.

In all three temptations, I believe the line of sight slips from its focus on God and attempts to bring our self into focus — to take ourselves too seriously; to take our spirituality too seriously; to take our ministry too seriously — to focus on ourselves instead of God. I think that is the core of the temptation that awaits you in the wilderness out there. The secular world will tell you boldly that it's all about you. But even the community of spirit — the good that we do — is the devil's playground.

This is powerfully acknowledged in the recent movie *The Devil's Advocate*. I wish I could recommend this movie to you because it carries a powerful message. But it also carries a well-deserved R rating, so I refer to it with some caution. The movie traces the life of a young southern U.S. lawyer who is spectacularly successful in criminal defense. His success leads to a dream position in New York City defending high profile criminals. As success piles upon success, we watch him being sucked deeper into the evil side of life and soon learn that his new senior partner is the devil himself. From beginning to end, the devil plays the young lawyer by appealing to his vanity — his self focus — his temptation to take himself and his work too seriously. In a dramatic struggle near the end of the movie, the lawyer takes his own life to prevent the devil from winning — only to find out that this was a daydream during a trial in his home town — a spark of conscience about his work as a small town defense lawyer — a burst of truth that causes him to walk out in the middle of the trial, to leave behind his sordid success. As he leaves the courtroom with his wife, proud of his courageous decision, a reporter asks for an exclusive interview. "This is a great story — a lawyer with a conscience. You will be a sensation!" The movie ends with the young lawyer agreeing to the interview and walking off as the reporter's face changes into the smiling face of the devil saying, "Vanity gets them every time!"

"Vanity gets them every time." Even when we choose the good — even when we do it for God we are vulnerable to the very human temptation to take ourselves too seriously, to allow our gaze to fall on our own image. When someone looks at our new faculty or our balanced budget and says to me, "Good job" and I stand up a little taller — I have just succumbed — and the devil smiles.

This is not to negate our self-esteem. Our value, our worth is established by God's love for us. The temptation is to shift our focus from the God who loves us to the object of God's love. A subtle but profound shift of focus that shapes the way we see everything else.

But Matthew tell us that when Jesus is tempted his response is consistent. Every time he deflects the focus from himself to God. Because for Jesus, even the wilderness, the place of temptation is still the sanctuary of God. It is where he is with God, and he never takes his eyes off of God.

Regent has been a sanctuary. Like the psalmist we needed to get away from the world and spend some time before God. This is a place where you have found perspective, where you have enjoyed the warmth of community, where your knowledge of God has been broadened and your walk with Jesus has been enriched. Now you are about to leave this sanctuary to go into a wilderness where everything is screaming for your attention — where your constant temptation will be *you.*

It is hard to leave this place, this community, these friends and mentors. But you do not go alone. This is God's world. He goes out on this pilgrimage with you. As the psalmist says, he has you by the hand.

Tomorrow, Aaron, my younger son, turns 29. He is an outgoing, highly relational young man. I think he was born relational — talkative and trusting! But we could have lost him. When he was two years old, a close friend and neighbor called him to come across the street to play with her son. With the invincible innocence of a two year old, Aaron charged into the street. At that moment a car turned abruptly into our quiet street — a woman in pain rushing to the dentist. Without warning there was the squeal of brakes and the car struck Aaron with its front bumper, spinning his little body around and throwing him under the car. Thankfully, the driver stopped with Aaron lying just in front of the rear wheels. It is one of those moments burned in our minds, but with gratitude to God. Aaron, with the resilience of the young, emerged from that hit with only a bad bruise and a healthy fear of streets. From that point on Aaron would not cross the street unless he held our hand. In fact he wanted to hold my hand wherever we went, across the street, on the sidewalk or on the mountain trail.

We started hiking and backpacking with the boys about this same time. And Aaron always held my hand. I remember his first hike at age two: a mile down into a canyon and, of course, a mile back up. His chubby little legs were wobbling by the time we reached the car but I wouldn't carry him. He had to do it on his own. And he did it, holding my finger all the way — needing the contact and encouragement. A father and a son connected by a tight sweaty grip on my finger as I held his hand. And that day we began a log book of all of our family hikes. By the time he was 10, Aaron had logged over 400 trail miles — probably holding my hand for most of them!

That's the image I have when I think about us leaving this sanctuary of God, the community of Regent College. Maybe we are on a trail into the wilderness, but God is near, he is our guide and he has us firmly by the hand.

As you leave this place — these friends and mentors — you leave a sanctuary of God, but you do not leave the people of God, you do not leave the presence of God. You do not go alone. You go out holding the hand of

God. Feel that grip and know that wherever you are, there God is.

May your focus always be on God. In the midst of the wilderness may you respond with the psalmist:

> *As for me, it is good to be near God.*
> *I have made the Sovereign Lord my refuge;*
> *I will tell all of his deeds.*

Regent Chapel
April 21, 1998

7

Theological Education at a Desert Well

*T*he Pharisees heard that Jesus was gaining and baptising more disciples than John, although in fact it was not Jesus who baptised, but his disciples. When the Lord learned of this, he left Judea and went back once more to Galilee.

Now he had to go through Samaria. So he came to a town in Samaria called Sychar, near the plot of ground Jacob had given to his son Joseph. Jacob's well was there, and Jesus, tired as he was from the journey, sat down by the well. It was about the sixth hour.

When a Samaritan woman came to draw water, Jesus said to her, "Will you give me a drink?" (His disciples had gone into the town to buy food.)

The Samaritan woman said to him, "You are a Jew and I am a Samaritan woman. How can you ask me for a drink?" (For Jews do not associate with Samaritans.)

Jesus answered her, "If you knew the gift of God and who it is that asks you for a drink, you would have asked him and he would have given you living water."

"Sir," the woman said, "You have nothing to draw with and the well is deep. Where can you get this living

water? Are you greater than our father Jacob, who gave us the well and drank from it himself, as did also his sons and his flocks and herds?"

Jesus answered, "All who drink this water will be thirsty again, but those who drink the water I give them will never thirst. Indeed, the water I give them will become in them a spring of water welling up to eternal life."

The woman said to him, "Sir, give me this water so that I won't get thirsty and have to keep coming here to draw water."

He told her, "Go, call your husband and come back."

"I have no husband," she replied.

Jesus said to her, "You are right when you say you have no husband. The fact is, you have had five husbands, and the man you now have is not your husband. What you have just said is quite true."

"Sir," the woman said, "I can see that you are a prophet. Our ancestors worshipped on this mountain, but you Jews claim that the place where we must worship is in Jerusalem."

Jesus declared, "Believe me, woman, a time is coming when you will worship the Father neither on this mountain nor in Jerusalem. You Samaritans worship what you do not know; we worship what we do know, for salvation is from the Jews. Yet a time is coming and has now come when the true worshippers will worship the Father in spirit and truth, for they are the kind of worshippers the Father seeks. God is spirit, and his worshippers must worship in spirit and in truth."

The woman said, "I know that Messiah" (called Christ) "is coming. When he comes, he will explain everything to us."

Then Jesus declared, "I who speak to you am he."

John 4:1-26

A new year begins. Or, more accurately, I should say, a new year continues, because this 27th academic year in the life of Regent College began with a flourish this summer. Before the dust of Convocation had even settled, and long before the faculty finished grading papers from last year, Summer School exploded into the college. The admissions and registration staff took one deep breath after graduation and were then submerged by wave after wave of students arriving on campus.

The summer program was kicked off with a week-long pastors' course attended by 250 church leaders. This should have warned us of the tidal wave that was on its way. From that day on, we welcomed record numbers of students and faculty all summer — students, like you, literally from around the world. Last week, before this fall term registration began, we had already enrolled over 1250 men and women in our summer courses. If the office staff looks tired—there is a reason!

This was indeed the summer for making waves. Those of you returning will remember the "cruise." Let me bring the rest of you up to date. We tried an experiment this summer. A tour company owned by one of Regent's board members sponsored a "Regent Alaskan Cruise" — seven days of comfort cruising the Inside Passage from Anchorage, Alaska to Vancouver, British Columbia, with Eugene Peterson as the morning Bible teacher. The purpose of this cruise was the promotion of Regent College — its educational programs and its investment opportunities — the promotion of Regent to a new constituency of people who did not know the College.

Forty-two persons registered for this unique, and expensive, summer school option. We represented about 8% of the passenger list on the cruise. We sailed for seven days, with five stops, at which, of course, I visited alumni and donors of the College! The cruise ended in Vancouver with a visit to Regent College where we attended the opening chapel of our largest summer session. For most of the travelers this was their first exposure to Regent. Only time will tell if this was a good fund raising event. On the other hand, it seems clear that we will see at least four or five of the participants here as students in the next few years. That alone may make the experiment worth doing.

But what stands out in my memory this morning is the reminder we had that it is God's program we are participating in. It is not our agenda that counts.

Because this cruise was partly a promotional trip, I went into it with a certain urgency to get alongside of people and work Regent into discussions

— probably to some extent to justify the decision to adopt this luxurious format. With some of the group it happened naturally; with others it was awkward, difficult and in some cases impossible. For the first three days of the trip, I was not really enjoying the scenery, or the relationships I was forming, because of my promotional agenda. I had come on this trip to recruit students and raise funds.

About day four I realized that I had it all wrong. This was not Regent's trip. This was not about my agenda. This was God's program in which we were participating. For the first three days I saw potential for Regent. From day four — I saw Leon, Sophia and Darlene. Leon was a professor of statistics who signed up for the cruise literally as his Regent summer school. He found Eugene's talks precisely the enriching Bible teaching that he was looking for. On day four, Leon met Sophia, an Australian woman cruising on vacation with her husband. When Sophia expressed appreciation for the wilderness beauty around us but lamented that her soul was thirsty, Leon invited her and her husband to Eugene's talk. As Sophia put it, this was a gift directly from God. She attended all the rest of Eugene's morning studies, drank up the information about Regent (that she got from Leon, not me), and asked me for information to give to her friends in Australia that she thought should come back with her to study at Regent. Later in the week, Sophia saw Darlene sitting alone in a corner of the cruise ship reading her Bible. Darlene was traveling the Inside Passage with her mother and trying to carve out a little space each day to sit before God. Sophia told her about Regent and showed up the next day at Eugene's talk with Darlene and her mother in tow, introduced them to Leon and asked me to tell them about Regent.

At this point, I had to admit: I had it all wrong. It was time to quit working the tour and relax into the relationships that God was setting up. This was not Regent's trip; this was not my agenda. This was God's program and we had a part to play in the story. And we may never know the full implications of our Alaskan cruise experiment. I think this cruise experience makes me more appreciative of the story in our text this morning: the woman going to the well for water.

She was a woman with an agenda, a person with a purpose. We only know a little about her. She must not have had an easy life. She was a Samaritan, a half-breed, a person with mixed blood lines. In the larger culture of Israel she was marginalized, victimized by a racism that made her untouchable. Even within the boundaries of Samaria she would not have complete peace. As a woman, her rights were limited and her self worth constantly challenged. And she was a woman who struggled with relationships, obviously unable to sustain the commitments of a healthy marriage. And she was out of water! Twelve o'clock — the heat of the day — and she has to go get water. Leaving the town and its problems behind her, she heads to the oasis carrying her empty water jar — a woman with an agenda, probably preoccupied with her own life as she walks the dusty path to Jacob's well. On the one hand, anxious to get the water and be done with this chore. On the other hand, in no hurry to return to the problems of daily life. So with the tangles of her life splashing around in the back of her mind, she heads straight to the well with one purpose — to get her water.

And she meets Jesus! She came for water. She found the Messiah. Her theological education has begun.

It may be stretching it a bit, but I see four truths in the woman's educational process that can be found in an academic community like Regent.

First, *theological education does not make life easier.* As she first began to learn about God she looks for an easier life. "Hmmm . . . if there is something here, maybe I won't have to keep coming back for water. Maybe life will be less difficult if I become a Christian. Maybe if I become part of a Christian community, people will take care of me, and I won't have such a hard life." But Jesus doesn't offer her such an easy out. His water will not keep her from having to work, from returning to the well in the heat of the day. It will not change the troubled environment in which she lives and to which she must return.

Second, *theological education is not about debating theology.* Like any good theological student, as soon as she realizes that her personal life is not necessarily going to be easier, she reaches for the dividing objectivity of truth, the debate over doctrine that separates people by their cognitive commitments. Theological schools can easily be filled with such polarizing debate, fracturing the community in the pursuit of truth, building the intellectual defenses that keep the One who is truth from penetrating the heart and igniting the love that unites the community. And again, Jesus acknowledges the differences in theological position between Samaritans and Jews but refocuses her attention on God and his presence with her right now.

Theological education is a relationship with God in Jesus Christ. Unfortunately at some theological institutions you might never get beyond the first two stages. At Regent however, we trust that God will lead us into that painful third stage that breaks down our defenses, that marginalizes our differences, that brings the unexamined life into the spotlight of God's loving gaze. And this is what Jesus offered the woman — the knowledge that he knew her — really knew her — knew all about her and still loved her. It is not easy to live in a relationship where every hidden secret, fear and failure is continually being exposed through the cracks in our carefully constructed facades. But that is what theological education is all about. It is about a relationship with God in Jesus in which we are known completely and thoroughly and loved anyway! Theological education is about an encounter with God that penetrates to the deepest core of our being and demands a response. Theological education is about truth and about relationship. It is in relationship with God that we learn the truth about ourselves. And it is often within the relationships of community that we understand the truth about God present.

And finally, *theological education is transformational.* When God has opened, entered and embraced the inner sanctums of your being, you are a different person. The Samaritan woman put down her pot and went back to town. She forgot her own agenda, why she had come to this well. She had met Jesus — the Messiah — and she needed to tell someone. She didn't go out to tell them how to get water more easily; she didn't go share with them the doctrine of worship that she had learned. She pointed them to God because of her relationship with Jesus. She put her personal agenda behind and found herself participating in God's program. People responded, the harvest began and the town of Sycar opened its doors to Jesus and its hearts to God. Many others found themselves confronted by God because a woman walked to the well to get water, encountered Jesus instead and began pointing people to God.

So — what about us? We sit here this morning beginning a new year of theological education. What brings you to Regent College this fall? What is your agenda this year? What water jar do you have in your hands?

You are entering an oasis, a community of the people of God in the midst of the churning sea of confused humanity, a breath of fresh air in a world that seems to be stagnating — a world filled with pain and problems. And like the Samaritan woman, we do not leave all of our troubles behind when we enter this community. We bring our hurts and wounds with us. We come to a community wanting to be cared for. And we enter a community filled with people who need to be cared for. We will focus on this directly at the Retreat this weekend, but let me make one comment about the paradox of community: a part of each one of us comes to this community wanting to be cared for. Thus, the people around you are in need of your ministry, of your caring.

Do not say "Four months more and then the harvest (or eight months more and then graduation). Open your eyes and look at the fields (look around you). They are ripe for harvest. You will find the community you seek only as you reach out in service to your neighbor. Community emerges out of caring relationships of service. It is always initiated by giving, not by waiting to receive.

Most of you have come to this year with an agenda, a set of expectations for God, for Regent, for the community. You may have come to learn the foundations of your faith, to build on the doctrinal truth that you believe. You may have come to sharpen your skills for ministry, to equip yourself for service in the church or the marketplace. You may have come to think through the integration of your faith with your life and work. Theological education includes all of this. This is in fact the water in this well.

But theological education at Regent College includes much more. Theological education is about a relationship with the living Christ. A relationship that will last a lifetime. A relationship that will strip away your protective masks and expose your soul to the love of God. God brought you here for a reason. So like the Samaritan woman, as this year begins set down your water jar. Lay your agenda aside. Sit by the well. Spend time with Jesus and point the people around you to God.

As we spend this year together, may we all have an encounter with God in Jesus Christ that transforms our living and results in relationships that care for one another and point people to God.

Regent Chapel
September 10, 1996

8

Leaving Bethel

*J*acob left Beersheba and set out for Haran. When he reached a certain place, he stopped for the night because the sun had set. Taking one of the stones there, he put it under his head and lay down to sleep. He had a dream in which he saw a stairway resting on the earth, with its top reaching to heaven, and the angels of God were ascending and descending on it. There above it stood the Lord, and he said: "I am the Lord, the God of your father Abraham and the God of Isaac. I will give you and your descendants the land on which you are lying. Your descendants will be like the dust of the earth, and you will spread out to the west and to the east, to the north and to the south. All peoples on earth will be blessed through you and your offspring. I am with you and will watch over you wherever you go, and I will bring you back to this land. I will not leave you until I have done what I have promised you."

When Jacob awoke from his sleep, he thought, "Surely the Lord is in this place, and I was not aware of it." He was afraid and said, "How awesome is this place! This *is none other than the house of God; this is the gate of heaven."*

Early the next morning, Jacob took the stone he had placed under his head and set it up as a pillar and poured oil on top of it. He called that place Bethel, though the city used to be called Luz.

Then Jacob made a vow, saying, "If God will be with me and will watch over me on this journey I am taking and will give me food to eat and clothes to wear so that I return safely to my father's house, then the Lord will be my God and this stone that I have set up as a pillar will be God's house, and of all that you give me I will give you a tenth."

Genesis 28:10-22

Jacob and all the people with him came to Luz (that is, Bethel) in the land of Canaan. There he built an altar, and he called the place El Bethel, because it was there that God revealed himself to him when he was fleeing from his brother.

Now Deborah, Rebekah's nurse, died and was buried under the oak below Bethel. So it was named Allon Bacuth.

After Jacob returned from Paddan Aram, God appeared to him again and blessed him. God said to him, "Your name is Jacob, but you will no longer be called Jacob; your name will be Israel." So he named him Israel.

And God said to him, "I am God Almighty; be fruitful and increase in number. A nation and a community of nations will come from you, and kings will

*come from your body. The land I gave to Abraham and
Isaac I also give to you, and I will give this land to your
descendants after you. Then God went up from him at the
place where he had talked with him.*

*Jacob set up a stone pillar at the place where God had
talked with him, and he poured out a drink offering on it;
he also poured oil on it. Jacob called the place where God
had talked with him Bethel.*

Genesis 35:6-14

He was born into a deeply religious immigrant family. His grandfather had come from the old country and launched the very successful family business. The stories about his grandfather are hard to believe. They say he was 100 years old when his second son was born. And that he nearly sacrificed that son in a passionate act of worship.

His father, perhaps because of his own experiences, was a quiet man, who married well from among his own people, who loved his two sons and enjoyed a good meal of wild game.

But his mother . . . now that's another story. She was a wise and cunning woman who believed deeply in the youngest of her twin sons and worked, even deviously, for his best interests. Not that he needed much help. He was his mother's son. Early on in the sibling rivalry between him and his brother, he bargained his hungry brother out of his legitimate birthright, guaranteeing his own financial future. And later, with his mother as co-conspirator, he tricked his aged father into giving him the family blessing, guaranteeing his future before God.

Of course, these behaviors did nothing to improve his relationship with his brother, and in wisdom his mother arranged for him to visit the relatives and look for a wife. And a wife he finds. But these are his mother's relatives . . . and now he knows where she got her cunning! In the world of his relatives, the rules keep changing. To get the wife he wants he ends up working 14 years on his uncle's ranch and has to marry her older sister first. Even then there is an attempt to cheat him out of his legitimate pay for the years of work he invested — 10 times the ground rules are manipulated and changed under his feet.

When he finally does free himself from the clutches of the relatives, he must confront the consequences of his youth. To return home he must face his brother — a thought that strikes terror in his heart. But again, things change in this world. His brother has done well in the family business and is a rich man, welcoming him with open arms and inviting him to live on the family estate. However, after 20 years with his unscrupulous uncle he has developed a healthy skepticism when it comes to relatives. So again, he deceives his brother — promises one thing but does another, choosing to separate himself from the family estate.

He's a survivor. A man who has learned to cope in a very human, often hostile and always changing world. Life is an unpredictable journey; the path keeps changing under his feet, and there is much more change yet down the road.

But one thing has not changed: the promise of God. A promise made to his grandfather and renewed with his father. A promise passed on in the blessing of his father. But more than that, a promise that was personalized in his own encounter with God. Jacob met God at Bethel — twice. First in a dream where the promise to the people of God was spoken directly to him. It was at Bethel that Jacob heard the words, "I am with you and will watch over you wherever you go." And it is from Bethel that God sends Jacob out "to be fruitful and increase in number", commissioning the people of God to become a blessing to the world. Between his arrival at Bethel and his sending out from Bethel, Jacob wrestled with God and was blessed by God, who in fact was with him, watching over him. Bethel is the place where Jacob encountered God and was transformed by the unchanging promise of God to be with his people and to watch over them wherever they go — the promise to be with Jacob as he leaves Bethel to live in a changing world.

And the world keeps changing. The Bethel experience did not smooth the path before him — it only assured him that God would walk the path with him. And it was a rocky path they walked. On the journey from Bethel, his wife Rebekah dies giving birth to his 12th son Benjamin. When he finally arrives at his father's house, it is just in time for Isaac's death, and Jacob buries him near his grandparents and his mother. Not long after that his son Joseph goes missing, presumably killed. And then there is the famine. No grain, nothing to eat, and he has to send his sons to Egypt to buy food, only to have Simeon arrested in Egypt. And then he discovers that Joseph in fact is a ruler in Egypt, sent ahead by God to prepare the way for his people. So, in another surprising change, Jacob is reunited with his lost son and moves his family to

Egypt — where he lives until his death, at which time he too is buried beside his parents and his grandparents.

I like the story of Jacob because I think it fits the reality of our life today. We live in a world that is in constant change. But we cling to a promise that God will walk with his people in the midst of this changing world. And at Regent — our Bethel — many of us have wrestled with God, encountered God anew as that promise becomes personal. And now you are being sent out from Bethel so that others may be blessed. A changing world. An unchanging promise. A personal relationship. A sending out — the journey of life.

The year is almost over. You are about to leave the comfort of this community and return to your corner of the world. You go out to change the world . . . or at least to make a difference in your part of the world as a servant of God, a disciple of Jesus Christ.

Change. Everyone is talking about it. It's happening all around us — whether we like it or not. It's happening within us. It's the same world in which Jacob lived, just spinning a little faster.

Most books on organizations and leadership today are focusing on change. Most books on church and ministry are talking about change. Most discussions of personal growth and survival are addressing change. Any move or transition in your life involves change. In a few days or weeks you will leave Regent and proceed to your various destinations; this is change.

Some of us like change. It is exciting! Most of us however are wary about change. Its uncomfortable — different. And it's happening way too fast! When I travel around and talk to people, the most common concern that I hear is the speed of change. People everywhere are struggling with the swirling change all around them. They are having trouble coping with a constantly changing world.

You go out into that world as participants in change, as persons who have experienced change in this time of learning and growth, but, more importantly, you go out as persons who have met God. You have spent time wrestling with the God who does not change and you can enter a changing world with confidence, continuing a journey with the God who holds the changing future in his hand — in fact with the God who participates in that future for his own purposes. You can face change because it does not change who you are at core — a person chosen and loved by God — the God who promises to be with you wherever you go.

Last week I spent two days in Toronto with the national leadership of

InterVarsity. Like most organizations, they are struggling to align their ministry and mission with a changing world. They gave me the topic: Leadership and Change. So we talked about coping with change. No one debates any more whether or not things are changing. We know they are — changing rapidly and continuously. The question is how we will respond to that change. So I gave them a little taste of Regent called "Take Two". You may recognize this as a game that Kirstin Jefferies, Bonnie Ma, Jude Fredricsen and Duffy Lott have introduced to the college community. They taught Beverly and me the game this year. Now, I am convinced that their motives for introducing this game are pure. For anyone foolish enough to challenge these women (who I am sure spend more time practicing than studying!) . . . anyone who enters their gladiatorial arena can sense their pure intentions immediately — total humiliation! Several of us on the faculty have fallen prey to these practiced competitors this past year. Yet there is always justice. What was intended as a game to blunt my competitive streak, I was actually able to incorporate into my class on leadership this spring and charge students tuition to play — revenge! Actually, I think the game illustrates an important reality in the world you are entering again.

In the game, you form crosswords out of scrabble tiles in timed competition with your opponents. When any player uses all their tiles in any form of crossword they shout "take two" and every player adds two more tiles to their personal supply to be formed into crosswords. With several good players, you are "taking two" more tiles faster than you can even think of words to spell with them. Most of us are sitting there with many unused tiles when Kirstin announces that she's done.

It's a fun, if frustrating, game but it illustrates two distinct approaches to change. For some players the first crossword formed becomes the defining strategy for the game and they struggle to fit the rapidly arriving new tiles into their original crossword. For others, with each shout of "take two," they see all of their tiles loose again and rethink a totally new crossword that can be formed out of the accumulated letters. One group seeks to extend strategies that work today into tomorrow's changed world. The other group looks for a new scenario for tomorrow that develops new strategies to account for the changed world.

Well, life is not as neatly defined as a game, but I do think there are some lessons here. As you go out around the world, hold on to the promise, invest in your relationship with God, keep your focus on being fruitful and increasing the people of God. This is a scenario or mission that may take a hundred forms in your life time. Don't cling to past strategies for church or for work or ministry just because they used to be important. Try to recognize the new tiles that God sends into your path and imagine the new future that you can live with them. Who knows what is ahead? God knows! And God has promised to walk creatively into that future with you. "Take two" with confidence.

I think this is of particular importance to Regent people because many of the motivations that brought you to Regent will not be fulfilled as deeply when you return to your church or marketplace community. Over and over again I hear Regent alums lamenting the difficulty of leaving Regent — leaving the Bethel where they met God — and returning to weak attempts at community by people preoccupied with the pressures of life. The church seems stale. The marketplace is consumed with survival. Relationships are superficial. There are few safe places in which to nurture your relationship with God, to share your walk with Jesus. The old strategies for Christian living are no longer fulfilling for many who have spent time with God at Bethel. This concerns me.

Over the years I have had most of you in my office for lunch or tea. We talked about why you came to Regent. There are many reasons, but several stand out. Some of you came to Regent to be part of a community that would nurture your spiritual growth. Some came seeking safe relationships in which to explore ideas and personal growth — a place to love and be loved. Some of you came expecting an encounter with God that would transform your lives. You came to worship. You came seeking a biblical foundation to undergird your faith, a theological framework for living in this world. Some of you want to think Christianly about all of life and work. Over and over I have heard these reasons for coming to Regent — and they are good reasons. But it troubles me. Almost every reason I listed does not require an educational institution to make it possible. In fact, I would argue that every one of these legitimate motivations should be addressed by the local church. The problem is — they aren't. Old structures and strategies are not serving adequately in a changing world. For the most part the church is not the safe communal learning center where people meet God. So you come to Regent, partly for its academic purpose — a diploma or degree, but partly because we are being used by God to do something I believe the church should be doing.

And now you return to that church, you have to survive in that market-place. And you are worried that the old strategies won't work for you. You have tasted a new way to live and learn together and that is what you will be looking for. Some of our alums leave the local church, some renew the church, some try to replicate Regent in their new context, some cannot cope.

I don't have any easy answers, but I would like to leave you with a challenge. I encourage you to look at the next stage of your life as a call to recreation. A call to recreate the church for the twenty-first century. I don't know if that means breathing life into old structures, or redefining church as little communities of theological education, or folding the church into the structures of the marketplace. But I do know that denominations, steeples, pews, organs, guitars, overhead projectors and perhaps even full-time paid ordained ministers are strategies. The church is the people of God. You are the people of God, and like Jacob you are being sent out as ambassadors of God to serve his people. Don't assume that the strategy and structures that you left should be defended and protected. Don't assume that Regent is the model that needs to be replicated. Regent also is only a strategy for today.

You have met God at Bethel. You have a personal promise that God will be with you and will watch over you wherever you go. And you are being sent out to be fruitful and increase the people of God. Look around you and see what pieces God is gathering. Create community wherever you go by risking yourself in the nurture of another's spiritual growth. Be a safe place for people to explore ideas and grow before God. Introduce them to the God of Bethel by the way you live and work, whether you herd sheep for 14 years, design computer software or renew the church. And teach what you have learned whenever you find people who want to learn. Recreate Bethel under the stars or in the middle of family struggles. Make Regent redundant.

Become a guide for people trying to find a solid path in a changing world. You can do all of that because you do not walk that path alone. You are the people of God. You have wrestled with God. And God has promised. He will be with you wherever you go. So leave this place where God has talked with you — go, be fruitful and increase in numbers. "Take two."

Regent Chapel
April 22, 1997

9

Encountering Jesus

*T*hey were on their way up to Jerusalem, with Jesus leading the way,
and the disciples were astonished,
while those who followed were
afraid. Again he took the Twelve aside and told them
what was going to happen to him. "We are going up to
Jerusalem," he said, "and the Son of Man will be betrayed
to the chief priests and teachers of the law. They will condemn him to death and will hand him over to the Gentiles,
who will mock him and spit on him, flog him and kill him.
Three days later he will rise."

*Then James and John, the sons of Zebedee, came
to him. "Teacher," they said, "we want you to do for us
whatever we ask."*

"What do you want me to do for you?" he asked.

*"They replied, "Let one of us sit at your right and the
other at your left in your glory."*

"You don't know what you are asking," Jesus said. "Can you drink the cup I drink or be baptised with the baptism I am baptized with?"

"We can," they answered.

Jesus said to them, "You will drink the cup I drink and be baptised with the baptism I am baptized with, but to sit at my right or left is not for me to grant. These places belong to those for whom they have been prepared."

"When the ten heard about this, they became indignant with James and John. Jesus called them together and said, "You know that those who are regarded as rulers of the Gentiles lord it over them, and their high officials exercise authority over them. Not so with you. Instead, whoever wants to become great among you must be your servant, and whoever wants to be first must be slave of all. For even the Son of Man did not come to be served, but to serve, and to give his life as a ransom for many."

Mark 10:32-45

What do you do when Jesus walks into your life?

We sit here this morning, a community gathered by God literally from around the world — people who have encountered the presence of God in Jesus and have chosen to come to Regent College to deepen our understanding of what it means to follow Jesus. We are here as followers, wanting to be equipped as leaders for the kingdom, as change agents who will make a difference in the world around us. We are not too different from James and John, the sons of Zebedee.

James and John were fishermen, working the Sea of Galilee on their father's boat, partners with Simon Peter and his brother Andrew. They worked hard to make a living and were good at what they did. They probably had heard stories of the new teacher in town, maybe had even heard him speak somewhere. They may well have heard suggestions that this new leader might be the Messiah their nation had been waiting for. Living under the harsh

Roman rule was quite oppressive. Maybe this man was the Messiah from God who would lead the people of Israel to freedom.

Then one day Jesus walks into their lives. Peter and Andrew, James and John had been out fishing all night with little success. It had been a hard night with out much to show for their efforts. As they are returning to shore to tie up their boats, they see Jesus talking to a crowd of people. People are pushing in all around him, trying to see him and hear his words. The fishermen tie up nearby where they can listen as they wash their nets. To their surprise, Jesus turns to them and asks if he can use a boat as a platform from which to speak, slightly out from shore where the crowd can see and hear him. He gets into Peter's boat and they anchor just off shore. And then Jesus teaches about the Kingdom of God. If James and John had not heard him before, they heard him now, close up. Jesus was in their world talking about God.

When Jesus finished, he turned to the fishermen and directed them to cast out their nets once more, even after their frustrating night. And as we know the story; the nets were filled with so many fish that both boats began to sink. They were astonished at the power of this person who entered their world and accomplished more with one directive than these professional fishermen had accomplished in a night of fishing! Maybe this is the leader we have all been waiting for.

When Jesus says, "Follow me," they follow. Peter and Andrew leave their boat with their companions, James and John leave their father and his crew and follow Jesus in what turns out to be an eye-opening adventure. In the next few weeks, as Mark tells us, they saw Jesus calm a storm with the authority of his words; they saw him heal a man possessed by demons; they saw him bring to life a little girl thought to be dead; they saw a woman healed by simply touching Jesus' clothes; they saw him feed large crowds of people with a few sack lunches; they saw him walk on water and they saw him heal the deaf, the mute and the blind. Clearly this man was not ordinary. This man possessed power from God to do things for Israel that no one had seen before.

Over the weeks, James and John along with Peter, became especially close to Jesus, selected by him as a kind of inner circle of friends among the 12 disciples. The intimacy of this relationship reached its height when Jesus took them with him to the mountain top where before their eyes he was transfigured and they heard the voice of God saying, "This is my son, whom I love. Listen to him." If there was any question in their minds, it was gone. Jesus was clearly a man sent from God. Peter said it for all of them, he was the Christ, the Messiah they had been waiting for.

The Jesus who had walked into their marketplace, entered their lives as fishermen, was sent here by God to establish the kingdom of God on earth. And they had been chosen by Jesus to help bring about that new kingdom. They followed him now with new intensity, listening to every word, struggling though to understand where his teaching about death and suffering fit into the launch of a new kingdom, but wanting to play their part, wanting to be change agents for the new kingdom that was about to break forth.

Like us, sitting here this morning, they were disciples of Jesus, following him, seeking to learn from him. At the feet of Jesus they pursued their theological education. They were there to be equipped as leaders for the new kingdom, bringing freedom to their people and God's rule to their nation. But they misunderstood what it means to be leaders in the kingdom, to be change agents in the world. And their misunderstanding can be instructive to us.

This comes through clearly in the passage we read this morning. James and John confident in the intimacy of their relationship with Jesus, wanting intensely to be used by God in the formation of his kingdom, in the calling of his people, bring the wrong set of expectations to their preparation as followers of Christ. They assume the Messiah will rule like a king, with officers and counselors of court. And that is not an unreasonable assumption. Their experience under Roman rule is one of kings and princes, caesars and senators, generals and armies. It is natural that they would anticipate a new kingdom coming into power with that same hierarchical military model of leadership. And they want to be part of that leadership team. They ask Jesus for the privilege to sit at his right and left in the kingdom court. They are seeking for themselves the senior positions of status and power in the new kingdom, positions from which they can have significant influence in bringing the kingdom rule to their people.

Perhaps we should give James and John the benefit of the doubt. Maybe they were not really thinking about status and prestige. Maybe they were only thinking of the good they could do with these positions of power. Unfortunately their colleagues are not as generous. Their fellow disciples see this request as a grab for power and they are angry. This is not the first time this topic has been discussed by the disciples. Mark tells us that earlier on a trip into Capernaum the disciples had been arguing over who was the greatest. And then as now, Jesus has to call them together, take their minds off of this differentiating, polarizing approach to leadership and power and return their focus onto him, teaching them the values of the new kingdom. Leadership in the kingdom of God is not about position or prestige. Being a change agent for Christ has little to do with status and role. These are human models not God's way of influencing people. Jesus explicitly dismisses this view. Kingdom leadership finds its power in service. Change will not be brought about by rule or authority, but by individual relationships of service, relationships in which our life is poured into the ones we seek to influence. The greatest persons in the kingdom of God will be the servants, those who invest their lives in the people around them not from positions of leadership but in relationships of service.

And Jesus offers himself as the model. Even the Son of Man, the Son of God does not come with position and authority from which to rule. Rather, he comes as a servant, investing himself in his people to the extent that he must die for their redemption.

This is a radical change of thinking for the disciples. James and John understood leadership as authority, giving directives, making things happen because you say so. They also like the adulation and recognition that accompanies this positional concept of leadership. Jesus, however, turns this model upside down. If we want to influence the world for change, if we want to provide leadership in the kingdom of God, we will become servants. We will offer our lives in relationships of service to those around us. Leadership in Jesus' kingdom is not about position. It is about relationship, about relationships of service that call for a life-giving investment in the people around us. Leadership has nothing to do with position or role. These are incidental opportunities in which to exercise servanthood.

James and John must have listened for they did become that kind of servant. They did become leaders of influence in the kingdom, and following the model of Jesus, they did pay for their service. James was executed by Herod Agrippa 10 years later, and we find John living in exile on Patmos Island 60 years later. They were servants who brought change to the world and paid a price for that privilege. They were not leaders whose authority was recognized and acclaimed, but servants who influenced the lives of those around them.

When we gather like this at the beginning of a new year, we come with the energy and enthusiasm of our call to follow Jesus, our response to the one who has entered our world and engaged us personally. We come seeking to be prepared as leaders of the kingdom, ambassadors for Christ. We want to make a difference in this world. We want to be agents of God for change in a world distracted by the busyness of living. And that is what theological education is all about. We see ourselves at Regent College participating in the transformational process that God has already begun when Jesus walked into your life. Your time at Regent is intended to prepare you to make a difference in this world, influencing those around you to see what God is doing in our midst. What we are about together this year is the building of relationships that allow us to be change agents in a world that has lost its way. We gather like this to focus on our relationship with God in Christ, seeking the intimacy of James and John. And we learn together how to build relationships of community that allow us to invest in the lives of those whom God places next to us. Making a difference in the kingdom starts with your relationship with God in Christ and then with your relationship with the person next to you. We are not about producing kings to rule, nor leaders to be placed on pedestals, nor drum majors to lead the parade. We are called to the task of encouraging service, producing men and women who invest in relationships to serve the people that God sends across their paths.

On the wall of the Getty Museum outside of Los Angeles, a painting arrests the eyes of visitors. *Christ's Entry into Brussels in 1889* startles the viewer with almost garish colors, depicting in surreal fashion a multitude of faces. This 1888 painting by the Belgian artist James Ensor is jarring is several ways. It stands out from the other paintings of its time. As one writer put it, "A pretty picture it is not. Painted at the time when impressionists were producing their most beautiful baby-pink-and-powder-blue pictures, Ensor's masterpiece anticipated by some 20 years the gaudy, emotion-charged movement that would come to be known as expressionism" (James O'Toole, *Leading Change*, Jossey-Bass, 1995, p.1).

The painting portrays a frenzied crowd of people flowing all over the street. It is a celebrating crowd, seeming as though everyone is doing their own thing. A chaotic party of self-interested diversity and variety. But where is Christ? Here again the painting jars most viewers who, based on most earlier paintings, look for the Christ to be leading the parade or centered in the picture. Ensor, however, places his Christ in the background, a little to the left of center, almost swallowed up by the crowd. This is not a picture of a Christ who dominates the scene. Rather, Ensor portrays a Christ that must compete against the multiple distractions of modernity. No one is paying any attention to the one who would be their savior. Everyone is caught up in his or her own living. No one is following Jesus.

James O'Toole, the Director of the Aspen Institute, called my attention to this painting. In his book, *Leading Change: Overcoming the Ideology of Comfort and the Tyranny of Custom*, O'Toole recognizes that Ensor has captured the reality of any who would be change agents in the world today. If we want to impact the world today, we cannot appeal to authority, position, status or sanctions. Like the Christ in Ensor's painting any change impact any leadership will have to begin with those closest. For the Christ of Ensor's painting to reach the people of Brussels, he will have to start with the people closest to him. He will have to get their attention and address their lives and needs. This, says O'Toole, is exactly where we must start today if we want to have an impact on this world. If we seek to be change agents, bringing the message of God to the world, we start with those around us. We get their attention by engaging them where they are. In that relationship, we have the opportunity to participate in their vision and growth. Leadership, says O'Toole, is not about position or status. It is about *relationships of respect*. It is about respect for people. It is about articulating a vision for life with them that they choose to follow because it has become *their vision*.

Ensor paints a picture over 100 years ago that captures the distractions of contemporary times and recognizes that position, authority and status do not mean much to the busy people of the marketplace. Even when truth stands in their midst, they are too caught up in their own agendas to see Christ present. As O'Toole suggests, it will only be through individual focused relationships that Jesus will get their attention and they will understand the truth of God's presence in their midst.

In many ways, as O'Toole notes, Ensor has captured the message that Jesus is teaching James and John. Followers of Christ in today's world will need to be servants of the people, investing in relationships that point to the truth of God's presence, not leaders marching at the head of the parade.

James and John saw the crowd — their country — in need of a leader. They saw Jesus, the Christ, the Messiah of God with the power to bring about the kingdom of God. They expected him to lead with authority and they wanted to share in that experience. But Jesus' response was radically different. He did not come to rule the crowd but to serve the people. As Ensor expressed in his painting, Jesus did not come to lead the people but to be in their midst. He came as a servant and gave his life for his people. Leadership in the kingdom of God is about relationships of service.

Like James and John, Jesus has walked into your life. He has entered your life in whatever you were doing and has called you to continue your theological education in walking with him. In that walk we have come together as the community of Regent College. Together we are about the process of theological education.

Theological education is about overcoming our distraction and, unlike the Brussels crowd in Ensor's painting, allowing ourselves to be engaged by the Christ in our midst. Theological education is about a relationship with God in Jesus Christ that shapes all of our relationships with those around us. Theological education is about relationships in community in which we serve one another and learn from each other. Theological education is about becoming more Christ-like, which means not becoming leaders of position but humble servants who give themselves to the people next to them and make a difference in this world.

We gather this morning, called to be leaders in the kingdom, ambassadors of Christ, change agents in the world. May God take all of us, like James and John, and shape us into his servants this year.

Regent Chapel
September 12, 1995

10

Launching on a New Adventure

*T*his is the text of the letter that the prophet Jeremiah sent from Jerusalem to the surviving elders among the exiles and to the priests, the prophets and all the other people Nebuchadnezzar had carried into exile from Jerusalem to Babylon. (This was after King Jehoiachin and the queen mother, the court officials and the leaders of Judah and Jerusalem, the artisans and the other skilled workers had gone into exile from Jerusalem.) He entrusted the letter to Elasah son of Shaphan and to Gemariah son of Hilkiah, whom Zedekiah king of Judah sent to King Nebuchadnezzar in Babylon. It said:*

"This is what the Lord Almighty, the God of Israel, says to all those I carried into exile from Jerusalem to Babylon: 'Build houses and settle down; plant gardens and eat what they produce. Marry and have sons and daughters; find wives for your sons and give your daughters in marriage, so that they too may have sons and daughters. Increase in number there; do not decrease. Also, seek the peace and prosperity of the city to which I have carried you into exile. Pray to the

Lord for it, because if it prospers, you too will prosper.' Yes, this is what the Lord Almighty, the god of Israel, says: 'Do not let the prophets and diviners among you deceive you. Do not listen to the dreams you encourage them to have. They are prophesying lies to you in my name. I have not sent them,' declares the Lord.

This is what the Lord says: 'When seventy years are completed for Babylon, I will come to you and fulfil my gracious promise to bring you back to this place. For I know the plans I have for you,' declares the Lord, 'plans to prosper you and not to harm you, plans to give you hope and a future. Then you will call upon me and come and pray to me, and I will listen to you. You will seek me and find me when you seek me with all your heart. I will be found by you,' declares the Lord, 'and will bring you back from captivity. I will gather you from all the nations and places where I have banished you,' declares the Lord, 'and will bring you back to the place from which I carried you into exile.'"

Jeremiah 29:1-14

In his letter to the Israelites living in exile far from their Jerusalem home, the prophet Jeremiah offers words of encouragement that may well ring true to your ears today as you prepare to leave this community, to launch a new adventure with God, to step into the future:

"For I know the plans I have for you," declares the Lord, "plans to prosper you and not to harm you, plans to give you hope and a future. Then you will call upon me and come and pray to me, and I will listen to you. You will seek me and find me when you seek me with all your heart. I will be found by you," declares the Lord. . . . (29:11-14)

Jeremiah's letter encourages the Israelites to relax and settle down while in

Babylon — with the promise that God will bring them home. They are the people of God — together they have hope and a future. Their adventure with God now begins in Babylon, but it is to be a journey home — a journey with God — whose presence will be with them — if they pray, listen and look for him.

I found these words helpful when the chapel committee came to see me a few weeks ago. They wanted to know what I planned to talk about today so they could prepare the service. The very fact that they scheduled the meeting caused me distress because, as I told them at that time, "I don't know what I am going to do, and it makes very anxious!" One of the committee members then, very wisely said, "That's a good title; most students will identify with it at year end!" — *I don't know what I am going to do, and it makes me very anxious.*

The year is over. Many of you will be leaving this community in a few weeks on a new journey, on a new adventure with God. New adventures can be exciting, but they also produce anxiety as unseen obstacles are imagined and big pieces of the future are not yet clear.

I remember well such an adventure with my friend Don. I like to think of myself as an outdoorsman. I have done a lot of mountain climbing, winter snow camping, cross country skiing and backpacking. A few years ago, Don talked me into going white water canoeing with him. He had canoed on many rivers in the eastern U.S. and assured me that he knew exactly what to do. All I had to do was come along and follow instructions.

So we planned a three-day trip for a 30-mile stretch of the East Carson River, running from central California into Nevada. He organized the equipment, planned the route, checked the water level and basically did everything. I came along for the ride.

As we packed the canoe along the river's edge, I commented that the water seemed to be moving rather fast! Don assured me that it would be no problem controlling the open canoe in this river. And besides, he noted, he had brought along the definitive book on canoeing, as well as a river map that explained what we would be encountering. *If* we ran into any difficult problems, we could stop and consult the book and map.

Somewhat calmed, I climbed into the front of the canoe, and was immediately alarmed again by the precariousness of my perch and the instability of the canoe even while we floated in calm water near the shore. About this time, a high mountain glacier with crevasses was sounding quite stable and secure compared to this swirling water. Again he spoke words of reassurance and we cast off into the river.

Immediately we were caught up in the current and swept downstream with icy water splashing into my lap with each bouncing wave. Don yelled at me to paddle to the left. I was worrying about staying in the canoe! He could paddle!

Swiftly the current rushed us downstream, but with each minute we were gaining confidence and some semblance of control — at least for the first seven minutes. Then we rounded the bend, got caught in an especially fast current and were being swept straight into a huge rock face stretching across half the river. Desperately we paddled, furiously attempting to get the canoe out of the current's pull and angling away from the rock face. But no such luck! We crashed head on into the rock face, swamped the canoe, rolled it over on top of us, dumped our poorly tied camping equipment into the river and soon found ourselves bobbing down the rushing river like corks help up only by our life vests.

I did not think I would drown, but as I watched our canoe and all my gear speeding downstream, I had visions of a very wet, very hungry, very long 30-mile walk to where our car would be waiting for us.

With the help of panic and the current, we scrambled to shore and discovered that God continues to watch over fools. Our canoe and all of our gear had been collected by a kayaker downstream and pulled to the shore to wait for us. My 30-mile walk was only 300 meters.

While Don tied the equipment in securely this time, I read the little map that explained the river. And what do you think I found? At the 10 minute mark was a big warning, in capital letters: "WATCH OUT FOR THE SLAMMER!" "Canoeists are advised to walk their canoe around this bend to avoid a major rock face overhanging the river." Now we find out!

With considerably less bravado, we coaxed our canoe down the river for several miles and then found a flat sunny area where we stopped early. The rest of the afternoon was spent drying out food, tent, sleeping bags and clothing, none of which had stayed dry in our waterproof canoe bags.

We also pulled out the definitive book on white water river canoeing, dried each page and proceeded to read about life in a canoe on a western white water river, particularly the chapter on disasters. It's never too late to learn!

With the knowledge we were able to derive from this time of study and humble reflection, we negotiated the remaining miles of the river over the next two days and finished the trip, exhilarated by the experience and the new level of skills we had obtained.

For me this story illustrates two truths that I often overlook. First, the knowledge or truth that I needed to help me negotiate the river was available if I was willing to pursue it. Someone had been there before us. We had the map. Someone had gone before and knew what the future held for us. But Don and I chose to ride on our limited knowledge in order to experience the adventure together. Well, we experienced the river, and I can tell you it is wet and cold!

Second, we were not alone. We were in the canoe together. Initially that didn't mean much since we had no coordination, rhythm or balance in our cooperation. But eventually we learned how to work together as my cries of panic evolved into constructive observations, and Don's shouted instructions actually meant something. By the end of the trip we were a team with precision maneuvers that impressed at least us.

Since that trip, I still have anxiety every time I climb into Don's canoe. And I have been dumped in the river enough times since then to justify my anxiety. But we have learned to trust each other and depend on the community of canoeists who often go with us. And we have yet to ride a river that has not been run by someone before us — someone does know what lies downstream.

Perhaps getting into that canoe and letting the current sweep us away is a little like leaving the solid ground of this community and launching out into a new adventure. It's not easy. This has been a holy place where you walked with God. It has been a fertile, nurturing community of caring relationships. It is not easy to leave this community, even though we know that the God who walks with us is the God who goes before us. He has plans for his people. He offers hope and a future, and he will be found in your future if you will seek him with all your heart. This is his river and we know where it goes. It leads to God. This adventure upon which you embark is a journey with God — along a route he has charted — a path Christ has already walked. If you look for God you will see signs of his presence all along the way.

And you do not go out alone. You leave this community with a room full of friendships — friends who are a postcard, telephone or e-mail message away. Maintain those relationships. Invest the time to keep in touch. Yet there is more. We leave this place with a network of friends, but we all belong to the people of God, and new friends, new relationships, a new community await you where ever God leads you, if you will seek him with all your heart. He will be found with his people.

Over Christmas I read again a little book given to me by Martha Zimmerman. *A Tree Full of Angels*, by Macrina Wiederkehr is a little gem. (See Chapter 1 above.) Sister Macrina is a nun, living in monastic communities, writing out of her life with God. She looks for and sees God in the ordinary things of daily living. I recommend this little book highly. She talks about the journey of life and the pain of leaving a community that you love.

Wiederkehr sees life as a journey, an adventure — a steady movement towards home. Home she sees as being with God — something we experience in part as we move in and out of communities, as we invest in and are nurtured by a lifetime of relationships. Life is a journey — a rapid river, if you will — that rushes us along from experience to experience, from person to person. It has its rocks and its white water, its calm eddies and its bubbling beauty. Because Christ has gone before, we know it flows home — there is hope and a future. It leads to the fully embracing presence of God — home.

But the message of this little book is more. Her eyes are not just on the horizon, the end of the journey. She savors the journey with its rapids and its relationships because she looks for God with all her heart — and she finds God in the ordinary things of life and living. She looks for God and sees the Holy in the ordinary — in the steaming cup of coffee, in the praising beauty of the desert poppy. God has gone before. He is already there. He offers hope and a future to his people. And she looks for him and finds God all around her.

She writes:

> When we walk to the edge of all the light we have
> and take that step into the darkness of the unknown,
> we must believe that one of two things will happen. . . .
> There will be something solid for us to stand on, or we
> will be taught to fly. [or swim!] (p. 150)

You are about to begin a new piece of your adventure with God as you launch into the river flowing through this community from the heart of God. You go to a world afraid of the future and desperate for hope. Paddle with the confidence that God has gone before you. Look for him everywhere; he is there. And look around you. There are others in the canoe. Add your gifts to theirs and learn to ride the river of life together.

You have a future and you have hope. A new thing is waiting to be done. May God be present with you forever.

Regent Chapel
April 23, 1996

11

Who am I?

*N*ow Moses was tending the flock of Jethro his father-in-law, the priest of Midian, and he led the flock to the far side of the desert and came to Horeb, the mountain of God. There the angel of the Lord appeared to him in flames of fire from within a bush. Moses saw that though the bush was on fire it did not burn up. So Moses thought, "I will go over and see this strange sight — why the bush does not burn up."

When the Lord saw that he had gone over to look, God called to him from within the bush, "Moses! Moses!"

And Moses said, "Here I am."

"Do not come any closer," God said. "Take off your sandals, for the place where you are standing is holy ground." Then he said, "I am the God of your father, the God of Abraham, the God of Isaac and the God of Jacob." At this, Moses hid his face, because he was afraid to look at God.

The Lord said, "I have indeed seen the misery of my people in Egypt. I have heard them crying out because of their slave drivers, and I am concerned about their suffering. So I have come down to rescue them from the hand of the Egyptians and to bring them up out of that land into a good and spacious land, a land flowing with milk and honey — the home of the Canaanites, Hittites, Amorites, Perizzites, Hivites and Jebusites. And now the cry of the Israelites has reached me, and I have seen the way the Egyptians are oppressing them. So now, go. I am sending you to Pharaoh to bring my people the Israelites out of Egypt."

But Moses said to God, "Who am I, that I should go to Pharaoh and bring the Israelites out of Egypt?"

And God said, "I will be with you. And this will be the sign to you that it is I who have sent you: When you have brought the people out of Egypt, you will worship God on this mountain."

Moses said to God, "Suppose I go to the Israelites and say to them, 'The God of your fathers has sent me to you,' and they ask me, 'What is his name?' Then what shall I tell them?"

God said to Moses, "I AM WHO I AM. This is what you are to say to the Israelites: 'I AM has sent me to you.'"
God also said to Moses "Say to the Israelites, 'The Lord, the God of your fathers — the God of Abraham, the God of Isaac and the God of Jacob — has sent me to you.' This is my name forever, the name by which I am to be remembered from generation to generation."

Exodus 3:1-15

This summer I was given a copy of Ernest Gaines' 1993 award-winning novel, *A Lesson Before Dying.* In this novel, Gaines sets forth a realistic picture of life in rural Louisiana in 1948. The story focuses on the relationship between two men, Grant and Jefferson. Grant is the local school teacher. Jefferson is a 21-year-old, poor, nearly illiterate, black plantation worker. Jefferson is in prison. He was the only surviving (and maybe innocent) participant in a liquor store hold up that resulted in the death of the owner and two of Jefferson's friends. The store owner was white. Slavery was now illegal, but segregation was the law and Jefferson was easily convicted by the all white jury. It is Grant's job to teach Jefferson *who he is* and *how to live* before the State of Louisiana executes him for murder. As the story unfolds, a small community of people — black and white — face three questions: *Who am I?, Who is God?* and *How do I live before I die?*

This summer, we participated in the funeral for Beverly's sister-in-law — a 46-year-old woman whose body just quit working. Three years ago the doctor gave her two years to live. She called us on a Monday to tell us she was going to die in a few days. She died on that Wednesday. The funeral service and the family gatherings were blendings of pain and joy as the story of Melinda's life was recounted from various perspectives. As people stared at the face of death, they withdrew into themselves and reflected on the same three questions that shaped the relationship between Grant and Jefferson: *Who am I? Who is God? What am I doing with my life?*

In the text that was read this morning, Moses stands before God with these same questions shaping what Martin Buber calls the Great Duologue. Moses left the palace of the Egyptian Pharaoh to find out who he was. In the search for his roots, Moses killed an Egyptian officer, came in conflict with his people and fled to the desert where he took up the life of a shepherd. As far as he is concerned, the search is over. He is not the Egyptian royalty he was raised to be, and he has experienced too much freedom to become a slave like his Hebrew people. So he settles with the nomadic family of Jethro, marries, raises a family and herds sheep. This is the context in which God reveals himself to Moses and lays out his expectations for Moses' life.

What we see in this passage is the beginning of the theological education of Moses. And I think there are some parallels that can be instructive as we begin a year of theological education together this week. Moses' theological education focuses on six questions: Where am I? Who am I? Who are you, God? What do you want me to do? What will you do? and Who will help me?

Theological education is about:

1. Understanding your context — Where you are.
2. Understanding yourself — Who you are.
3. Understanding theology — Who God is.
4. Understanding your role — What God expects from you.
5. Understanding God's role — What you can expect from God.
6. Understanding community — What you can expect from those around you.

This morning I want to look briefly at the first three components of Moses' theological education. At our closing chapel this spring (Chapter 7), I want to look at the last three.

First, theological education is about understanding your context, knowing where you are. Moses was out feeding his flock on the slopes of Mt. Horeb when he sees a bush on fire but not burning. This curiosity attracts his attention and a voice tells him that he is on holy ground. Two things strike me in this beginning. First, who starts this educational program? Second, what is holy?

Moses is out doing his job; he is not looking for trouble and he is not looking for God. God appears in the bush and God speaks to Moses. *Theological education is about God who reveals himself, not about our search for God.* With all the energy and excitement of preparing for a year of study here in Vancouver, it is easy to bring theological education down to our agenda. Like everything else in our secular society, we want to bring the transcendent God into the confines of curriculum and the certainty of knowledge. We are here to study; we are here to learn about God, we are here to learn how to live before dying. And yet, Regent College is no more than a bush on fire not yet burned up. It is a place to which you have turned off in curiosity and, we trust, a place where you will hear the voice of God. It is not our search for education that counts; it is the reality and the hope that God has revealed himself and will continue to reveal himself to you in the year ahead.

But what is this holy ground? I would guess that the soil of Mt. Horeb was no different before, during or after this dialogue. What made this ground holy was the presence of God. *Where God is with you is holy ground.* Regent College is holy ground. Not because of any special characteristics of this place, this community — but because God is present in our midst. You have come to the mountain and you should expect to meet God.

I find myself often speaking about what I call "the culture of expectation" at Regent. We come to this community expecting to meet God — and we do. There is an expectation here that God is present and that he will meet you during your time at the college. You come with that expectation, the faculty and staff have that expectation, and for the past six years I have been here, I have watched it happen. I expect you to meet God this year in a way that will change your life forever just like Moses. This is holy ground. And wherever you go from here with God is holy ground. Holy ground is about your relationship with God. Leave your sandals in the closet because I hope you walk on holy ground all of your life. *Theological education is about understanding your context,* that you are in the presence of the God who reveals himself to you and walks with you on holy ground.

Second, theological education is about understanding yourself. Like Moses, each one of us is a story of God at work. Over these next few weeks you will be invited to share your story as you become part of the story of the community of Regent College. This is both good and bad. It is bad to the extent that it feeds the popular thinking that our story is all that is important. We live in a culture that worships the self and wants to bring all of experience under the critique of "my story."

On the other hand, God is forming a community again this year at Regent College and the sharing of personal stories is a reminder that together we participate in the story of Regent College, and this year is only one piece of the story of God at work in this world.

Each of us enters this story with some anxiety. We know our own story only too well. We know our limitations as well as our abilities, our fears as well as our joys and our failures as well as our successes. What we contribute to this community — how we fit into God's work — is not always clear at the beginning of a new year. Most of us enter the process of theological education — indeed all of Christian ministry — with the question: *Who am I* that I should be about this work with God?

This was the first thought that jumped into Moses' mind. Who am I that I should go to Pharaoh? Moses knew his limitations well. Talk about a troubled life! He was abandoned as a child by a mother who knew that she could not care for him and keep him alive in her current situation. Discovered before any harm could come, he was adopted by a prominent wealthy family of a different race. Loved and cared for, he was educated in the best schools and equipped to be a leader. And yet he knew he didn't belong. He was different.

Drawn by some inner compulsion, he started visiting the ghetto community that birthed him. The contrast between the life of "his" people and the genteel life that had been his in the palace was overpowering. Injustice and violence ruled in the ghetto community.

One day as he watched an officer abuse one of his people, something snapped. He tried to intervene, but it escalated to violence. Before he realized what had happened, he killed the officer! Thinking quickly, he hid the body and removed the evidence. Life was cheap in the ghetto and it was unlikely the death could ever by traced to him. But he had no peace. Living in luxury with blood on his hands, he found himself continually drawn back to the ghetto community, walking the streets of despair. He could not break away.

Then again violence erupts, injustice strikes. This time it is one of his own people preying on one of his people. What a waste. He steps in to break it up and is surprised to see them both back off, saying things like: "It's the murderer!" "The police are after him." "Get out of here before he kills us."

With that warning, he runs as fast and as far as his resources will take him. An abandoned child, adopted into luxury, now a fugitive. His feeble attempts to help his people have ended in failure and he is forced to flee. He leaves the country and goes to a rural setting where no one will know who he is and starts a new life as a shepherd.

For 40 years he wandered the deserts of Midian with the sheep. Not a lot of use for his great education or his leadership training. (Although some might argue that there is considerable similarity between leadership today and sheep farming! Leaders today try to keep the flock moving in the same direction and keep the strays from losing sight of where the flock is going.)

Moses — abandoned baby, adopted prince, educated leader, fugitive killer, veteran sheep farmer. That's the man who meets God on Mt. Horeb! And that's the tangled life — the Mosaic, if you will — of conflicting experiences packaged in one flawed human that God will use.

Is it any wonder that Moses asked: "Who am I that I should go to Pharaoh to bring my people the Israelites out of Egypt?" A legitimate question from Moses' perspective.

And if you read the full story of Moses' life and leadership, you realize that he is never freed from this question. When he is not asking the question someone else is! "Who do you think you are, Moses, to lead us in this way?" From beginning to end, Moses' leadership is challenged by the Israelites and those closest to him: "Who do you think you are to speak for God?" A legitimate question and one probably familiar to all of us . . . but *it's the wrong question!* From God's perspective Moses is good enough. God intends to use Moses just as he is — with his strengths and his weaknesses — both of which Moses will stumble over as he seeks to carry out God's direction.

We bring the full spectrum of stories into the community of Regent this year. In each life God has been working. We will learn together and grow together as God works in our midst. Who you are is good enough for God!

Who am I? is the wrong question. The more important question is Moses' next one: *Who are you?* It is not who am I that matters . . . it's *Who is God?* This is the heart of theological education. *Theological education is about understanding theology, understanding who God is?*

There is much we could talk about in the exchange between God and Moses that centers on this question. Moses was probably genuinely concerned that the Hebrews would not know who he was talking about when he said he was speaking for God. However, it is also possible that Moses wanted a little control over God as he reached for the intimacy of the divine name and looked for some miraculous signs to show that he could call up the power of God when he needed it. It is this latter temptation that comes back to haunt him at the rock at Meribah and ultimately prevents him from entering the promised land of Canaan.

This may be the ultimate temptation and danger in theological education — the temptation to think that we can possess God, to know God intimately and completely through our studies, to capture Christ in our classrooms, to define the Trinity in our curriculum, to encompass the holy in chapel, to use the power of God to credential our ministry. Theological education is about understanding who God is. . . . and the little that we can understand should drive us to our knees in awe! The transcendent God who will reveal himself to you this year cannot be packaged in a degree program or awarded at Convocation. The presence of God means the absence of control — it means obedience and service.

In this dialogue between Moses and God, we do learn some things about God. As we have already noted, he is the *one who reveals himself.* He is also the *one who has been there.* Moses was instructed to tell the Israelites that he spoke for the God of their fathers, the God of Abraham, the God of Isaac, the God of Jacob. He was to rekindle their memories. God has been there in their captivity, from their beginnings.

As Jefferson faced death in *A Lesson Before Dying*, and Melinda said goodbye to her family this summer, both knew that God had been there, that in Christ a path had been paved through the wildness of death. The God who reveals himself is the God who has been there and is with us now.

And more, he is the *God who will be there.* Because he has been there in their past, the Israelites can count on the reality that he will be there in their future. He will keep his promises — the promises that he made to Abraham, to Isaac and to Jacob. He will keep his promise to deliver them out of Egypt and to lead them into a land that will be their own.

This is the God you will encounter this year. A God who reveals himself — a God who has been there in the past, even in your past — a God who will be there in the future, including the immediate future of your year of study at Regent. Part of what theological education is about is remembering — remembering what God has done in history as the prerequisite to his work in our midst today and tomorrow. The story that you bring with you is your assurance that God will be in our midst this year.

Theological education at its best is about an encounter with God — the deepening of a relationship with the God we seek to serve and obey. That is what this year together is all about. Many of us come to the task of theological education in appropriate humility asking, "Who am I?" But as Moses found out, that's the wrong question. It points the wrong way. It is not Who am I? that matters. *It's who is God?* Theological education is about God revealing himself to you and in that revelation understanding more clearly who you are and that wherever you are with God is holy ground.

We enter this new year with high expectations. We expect to meet God; we expect to learn and to grow individually and corporately. We expect to be transformed by this time together. As you begin this new year, is your expectation shaped by who you are or by who God is?

Regent Chapel
September 13, 1994

12

So Now, Go and
Bring My People Out!

*M*oses answered, "What if they do not believe me or listen to me and say, 'The Lord did not appear to you'?"

Then the Lord said to him, "What is that in your hand?"

"A staff," he replied.

The Lord said, "Throw it on the ground."

Moses threw it on the ground and it became a snake, and he ran from it. Then the Lord said to him, "Reach out your hand and take it by the tail." So Moses reached out and took hold of the snake and it turned back into a staff in his hand. "This," said the Lord, "is so that they may believe that the Lord, the God of their fathers — the God of Abraham, the God of Isaac and the God of Jacob — has appeared to you."

Then the Lord said, "Put your hand inside your cloak." So Moses put his hand into his cloak, and when he took it out, it was leprous, like snow.

"Now put it back into your cloak," he said. So Moses put his hand back into his cloak, and when he took it out, it was restored, like the rest of his flesh.

Then the Lord said, "If they do not believe you or pay attention to the first miraculous sign, they may believe the second. But if they do not believe these two signs or listen to you, take some water from the Nile and pour it on the dry ground. The water you take from the river will become blood on the ground."

Moses said to the Lord, "O Lord, I have never been eloquent, neither in the past nor since you have spoken to your servant. I am slow of speech and tongue."

The Lord said to him, "Who gave human beings their mouths? Who makes them deaf or mute? Who gives them sight or makes them blind? Is it not I, the Lord? Now go; I will help you speak and will teach you what to say."

But Moses said, "O Lord, please send someone else to do it."

Then the Lord's anger burned against Moses and he said, "What about your brother, Aaron the Levite? I know he can speak well. He is already on his way to meet you, and his heart will be glad when he sees you. You shall speak to him and put words in his mouth; I will help both of you speak and will teach you what to do. He will speak to the people for you, and it will be as if he were your mouth and as if you were God to him. But take this staff in your hand so that you can perform miraculous signs with it."

Then Moses went back to Jethro his father-in-law,
and said to him, "Let me go back to my own people in
Egypt to see if any of them are still alive."

Jethro said, "Go and I wish you well."

Now the Lord had said to Moses in Midian, "Go back
to Egypt, for all those who wanted to kill you are dead."
So Moses took his wife and sons, put them on a donkey
and started back to Egypt. And he took the staff of God
in his hand.

Exodus 4:1-20

It's Midian several millennia ago. A lonely shepherd wanders with his sheep along the slopes of Mt. Horeb. Suddenly a bush bursts into flame — burning brightly but not burning up. As the shepherd moves cautiously toward the bush . . . it speaks. Out of the flames comes the voice of God calling him by name: Moses. And thus begins the famous duologue in which God takes a fugitive shepherd, hiding in guilt from a murder he committed in Egypt, and sends him back to that world to bring out the people of God.

Now, if I were Jeremy Begbie, this would be a good place for an audio or visual demonstration. Dal Schindell suggested setting fire to the podium . . . but we'll probably need it for summer school.

Last September, I talked about this burning-bush encounter between Moses and God, and drew parallels to the encounter with God that occurs in theological education as we enter the holy ground of God's presence and learn who we are in the context of learning who God is. Now the year is over and you are being sent back to bring out God's people.

It is fitting that we end our year immediately following Easter. This weekend we gathered to reflect again on our encounter with God in the life, death and resurrection of Jesus. It was a time to stand again before our burning bush — the cross. As we linger at the cross with the glow of Easter hope still warming us like a fire close by, we end this year and leave this community with God's command to Moses still before us: "Now, go . . . and bring my people . . . out!"

That's what theological education has been all about — preparing you to go and point people to God — to lift their spirits from the preoccupation of life and show them the way across the desert to the presence of God — to a burning-bush-understanding of life — a cross-shaped hope for tomorrow.

Like Moses, I hope we leave our encounter with God this year with an understanding of what God expects from us, with an understanding of what we can expect from God and with the realization that we are one piece of a larger community of called people.

What God Expects from Us

What *does* God expect from us? The mission statement of Regent College suggests that we have been preparing you as leaders — men and women whose very lives will point to God, modeling what it means to bring all of human life under the Lordship of Christ and demonstrating wherever you go the saving grace of God. A rather awesome calling!

And that's how Moses felt! "Who am I?" he asked. And God said, "Wrong question, Moses!" The right question is "Who is God?" And to this question God answers, "The one who will be with you." That is the question and the answer we need as we leave this community and go out to the people of God.

Aaron Wildavsky has written a provocative book entitled *The Nursing Father*, a study of Moses as the political leader of his people. Moses begins as a passive vessel for God's work and becomes a covenant intermediary between God and his people. Yet the entire journey is a struggle for Moses. From the beginning he does not want to go. He feels weak and under qualified. He lacks the gifts for this assignment. But God still says "Go!" He has not yet learned enough. But God still says, "Go!" Time after time Moses struggles to keep the Hebrews' attention focused on God — sometimes succeeding, sometimes enduring their complaints and attacks, sometimes getting himself confused with God, regularly returning to God in frustration looking for help or release from his calling. As Wildavsky puts it,

> Though Moses is called to lead, his subsequent trials derive in part from the desire to escape from responsibility by getting God to give him a "How to Do It" leadership handbook. The Israelites murmur to

Moses, and Moses calls for divine advice. The answer is
unrelenting: "Try".

(Wildavsky, *The Nursing Father,* p. 212)

Like Moses, you leave this place knowing how much more you need to
know, how much more you have to learn, how much deeper your faith should
be, how fragile and vulnerable you are. But also like Moses, you hear the
words, "Go! Try! I will be with you." And it is these *final* words that you can
hold on to with confidence. It doesn't matter how strong or weak you think
you are. I hope you take from your time at Regent College one thing: the
understanding that God intends to be with you. *God* will do *his* work through
you if you will but go and try.

What we can expect from God

This is our expectation as we leave this community. God will be with
us. He will do his work in us, through us and in spite of us. We believe this.
But sometimes its hard to see or remember when the task ahead looks overwhelming — when the future is too ambiguous. We believe it in our hearts,
but we wrestle with it in our minds and our feet do not always want to keep
on walking when we can't see what's ahead. But God says "Go! Try! I will be
with you."

Working with the passage, I have often struggled with God when it
feels like I am being sent into something too big, something beyond my
ability, something too hard or too painful to handle. I can't do it. I almost
get angry that I have to go out and pick up the responsibility with all of my
own fears and personal limitations. And I am jealous of Moses! At least he
had three miraculous signs that God was with him. His staff turned into a
snake; his hand could become diseased; he could turn Nile River water into
blood! Where are my three signs? A few miracles like that would significantly
enhance my leadership!

One day, while walking on the beach, struggling with God about leadership and limitations, a thought struck me. Maybe a thought from God, maybe
my own fantasies, maybe some mixture of both. God offers me, and you, the
same thing he gave Moses: the reminder of three things he can use, and the
realization that they are not so unique.

Three things that God can use for his purposes. A shepherds staff, a healthy body and river water.

A staff that becomes a snake. Perhaps the significance of the staff is not in the fact that it could become a snake, but in the recognition that God can use the tools of one's trade, whatever that may be. The common ordinary day-to-day tool of the shepherd became an instrument for God's power. Can we draw a parallel here to our own situations? Can God use the experiences, training and equipment of your work, coupled with the knowledge and skills acquired during your study at Regent, as instruments of his power? What are the accouterments of your trade, the abilities and talents of your profession, the skills and knowledges of your work? It seems to me that God is showing Moses that these are the things he will use for his work in the world, if we will but "Go, and try". The God who goes with us takes up the realities of our work and sanctifies them for his use.

A healthy body that can become diseased. This particular miracle has never appealed to me as much as the other two, but here it is. And again, God is using something ordinary and common to show his power — the physical health and energy of the person. Whether the hand is strong or diseased, God can use it to make his point. Perhaps God is reminding Moses, and me, and maybe you, that our very life, breath and health is a gift from God — a gift to be made available for his service — a gift that he can use as an instrument of his power in this world. Nothing exciting, nothing dramatic. Simply the breath in my body and my current state of health, such as it may be, is something that God will use for his work in the world, if we will but "Go and try." The God who goes with us takes up the frail frame of our humanity and hallows it for his use.

River water that turns to blood. Perhaps I'm stretching this one a little, but it strikes me that the Nile river was the primary resource of this desert area. It provided the irrigation for crops, the water for drinking, washing and a means of transport. Again, God is using something ordinary and common to show his power — the resources and assets available at the moment. Nothing unique to Moses, nothing unique to God. Simply taking the resources that were present and using them as an a instrument of God's power. Perhaps wealth, perhaps knowledge, perhaps connections or relationships. Perhaps geography, perhaps technology. Perhaps it does not really matter. Wherever you find yourself, whatever environment you are in, the resources at hand are all instruments for God's use, if we will but "Go and try!" The God who goes with us takes up these resources and assets and blesses them for his use.

It seems to me that what God is saying to Moses, and to me and you, is "Go . . . and I will go with you. I will be there in your work; I will be there in your living; I will be there in your various environments. My power *will* be manifested in you, now go and be my servant."

The miracle is not in the work, the living or the place, it is in the presence of God. Even for Moses they were not really one-of-a-kind miracles. All of the spiritual leaders in Pharaoh's court could the same thing. Hardly convincing proof that God's power rested on Moses. The power comes in making them available to God. The power comes from the presence of God that turns your place, your work, your living into holy ground. Let your work become a place where God is served. Let your living and dying be a demonstration of God's grace. Recognize that wherever you are with God is holy ground.

The Community of God's People

One more point needs to be noted in this passage. We know that we do not go out alone. God promises to go with us. But there is more — a further concession to Moses' fears and limitations. God sends Aaron along with him, to do those things that Moses is not very good at. I find great comfort in this fact.

None of us are ready or equipped to do it all. At best we can stumble forward in our limitations and offer what we have in God's service. We need help . . . and that is part of the promise. Even Moses needed help. He needed Aaron to do his talking. He needed Aaron and Hur to hold his arms up while Joshua was fighting his battles. He needed leaders to help him judge; he needed elders to help him lead. As Wildavsky says, "It is not Moses that is being called out at the burning bush, it is the people of God" (Wildavsky, p. 172). Moses goes out as one member of God's people to offer himself in God's service and he needs the other gifted members of that people to do what he cannot do.

You leave Regent College at the end of this academic year to return to your communities, your work, your family and friends. You go out to serve. But you do not go out to serve alone. The people of God are out there as well as in here. They are waiting for your gifts, your knowledge, your passions, your visions, your hopes. And they are ready for your fears, your doubts, your weaknesses, your uncertainties. You go out as one person in the community of God's kingdom, one member of the people of God, a little more equipped, a little better educated — a person with something to offer — and a person needing help. Surround yourselves with the community of God's people and engage your life of service out of the context of that community. God will do what he wants to do through you and God will raise up other people through whom he will do the rest.

You have been called to a life of service in the name of the resurrected Christ, "Now go . . . and bring out the people of God."

Regent Chapel
April 18, 1995

13

Great Expectations

*I*t was just before the Passover Feast. Jesus knew that the time had come for him to leave this world and go to the Father. Having loved his own who were in the world, he now showed them the full extent of his love.

The evening meal was being served, and the devil had already prompted Judas Iscariot, son of Simon, to betray Jesus. Jesus knew that the Father had put all things under his power, and that he had come from God and was returning to God; so he got up from the meal, took off his outer clothing, and wrapped a towel around his waist. After that, he poured water into a basin and began to wash his disciples' feet, drying them with the towel that was wrapped around him.

He came to Simon Peter, who said to him, "Lord, are you going to wash my feet?"

Jesus replied, "You do not realize now what I am doing, but later you will understand."

"No," said Peter, "you shall never wash my feet."

Jesus answered, "Unless I wash you, you have no part with me."

"Then, Lord," Simon Peter replied, "not just my feet but my hands and my head as well!"

Jesus answered, "Those who have had a bath need only to wash their feet; their whole body is clean. And you are clean, though not every one of you." For he knew who was going to betray him, and that was why he said not every one was clean.

When he had finished washing their feet, he put on his clothes and returned to his place. "Do you understand what I have done for you?" he asked them. "You call me 'Teacher' and 'Lord,' and rightly so, for that is what I am. Now that I, your Lord and Teacher, have washed your feet, you also should wash one another's feet. I have set the example that you should do as I have done for you. I tell you the truth, servants are not greater than their masters, nor are messengers greater than those who sent them. Now that you know these things, you will be blessed if you do them.

"I am not referring to all of you; I know those I have chosen. But this is to fulfil the scripture: 'He who shares my bread has lifted up his heel against me.'

"I am telling you now before it happens, so that when it does happen you will believe that I am He. I tell you the truth, whoever accepts anyone I send accepts me; and whoever accepts me accepts the one who sent me."

After he had said this, Jesus was troubled in spirit and testified, "I tell you the truth, one of you is going to betray me."

His disciples stared at one another, at a loss to know which of them he meant. One of them, the disciple whom Jesus loved, was reclining next to him. Simon Peter motioned to this disciple and said, "Ask him which one he means."

Leaning back against Jesus, he asked him, "Lord, who is it?"

Jesus answered, "It is the one to whom I will give this piece of bread when I have dipped it in the dish." Then, dipping the piece of bread, he gave it to Judas Iscariot, son of Simon. As soon as Judas took the bread, Satan entered into him.

"What you are about to do, do quickly," Jesus told him, but no one at the meal understood why Jesus said this to him. Since Judas had charge of the money, some thought Jesus was telling him to buy what was needed for the Feast, or to give something to the poor. As soon as Judas had taken the bread, he went out. And it was night.

John 13:1-30

At the end of the refectory of the Monastery of Santa Maria delle Grazie, in Milan, a painting stretches from wall to wall. In a hall designed for eating, the painting captures a moment in the life of 13 people gathered around an evening meal. Twelve men awaiting a word from their leader, waiting expectantly for him to reveal which one of them will betray him to the guards out looking for him that very day. Thought by many to be the most famous painting in the world, Leonardo da Vinci's *The Last Supper* captures the psychological moment that Jesus says to his disciples, "One of you shall betray me."

Twelve men are portrayed on canvas as Leonardo seeks to explore the turmoil and self-searching that was going on in each mind. "Is it I?" Each of them had chosen to follow this young leader for personal reasons that compelled them to leave their work and commit their destinies into his hands.

As they had lived with him and watched him each day, their expectations had been reworked as he patiently and continually refocused their thinking toward his appointed death and subsequent resurrection. Even as this dinner unfolds it becomes clear that his messianic leadership is heading to the cross, not to the uprising and reasserting of the nation of Israel that many expected. And we know that when the end appeared no one was really ready. They are all caught by surprise; their expectations reeling. Even Peter who enthusiastically proclaimed that Jesus is, in fact, the Christ, still wanted to stop the arrest by fighting, and denies knowledge of his Lord to save his own skin. Twelve men following Jesus with their own personal set of expectations, struggling to realign their expectations with the new agenda that Jesus is showing them.

And now he is piercing to the very heart of their struggle. "One of you shall betray me!" Each one looks at Jesus, remembers why he chose to follow, searches his own doubts and weaknesses and wonders, "Is it I?"

For many around that table, there was a crisis of expectations. But for one that crisis had already erupted into action. Judas had already decided that Jesus was failing to live up to his expectations and had begun the process of taking matters into his own hands.

This summer I picked up a little book by Leo Perutz, a Czechoslovakian writer and mathematician. In his last novel, *Leonardo's Judas*, completed just days before his death, Perutz portrays Leonardo Da Vinci resisting completion of his commission to paint *The Last Supper*. According to Perutz, the delay is caused because Leonardo cannot find a suitable face with which to depict Judas at this dramatic dinner.

Leonardo's search brings him into contact with Joachim Behaim, a German businessman in Milan on business. Behaim is obsessed by competing forces. He is madly in love with a beautiful young Milanese woman, Niccola, and furiously angry with a crafty money lender in Milan who has cheated him out of a moderate amount of money. It was a quest for this money that brought him to Milan in the first place. As these two story lines unfold in the novel, Behaim falls more deeply in love as Niccola returns his passion and makes plans to take her away as his wife. At the same time his anger escalates to violence as he unsuccessfully attempts to regain his money. Well, the reader realizes long before Behaim, of course, that Niccola is the daughter of the dishonest banker. The novel ends with the painful intersection of these two story lines, bringing violence to the community of Milan, justice to the crooked money lender and the betrayal of Niccola by Behaim.

At this point Leonardo walks into the scene and sees before him a man who is still deeply in love, but whose disappointment and pride will not let him express his love. As Behaim puts the money he was owed in his purse and prepares to leave Milan alone, Leonardo Da Vinci sketches his face and Behaim becomes the Judas of *The Last Supper*.

He loved her so much he had to betray her so she would not dissuade him from his primary objective. He was afraid he would love her *too* much and lose his obsession for his personal business agenda. Leonardo and Perutz call this pride.

Years later when Niccola again sees Behaim, she comments to a friend, "I could never have loved him if I had known that he had the face of Judas!"

Judas — one who expected so much from Jesus — one whose personal agenda so dominated his thinking that he was incapable of refocusing on what God was in fact doing. Judas was a zealot. He longed for the freedom of his people, for the restoration the independence and power to Israel. His whole life was committed to breaking the yoke of bondage that Rome had placed upon his country.

When the young teacher Jesus appeared, Judas' hopes soared. Like James and John, he saw that here was a leader the people would follow. This one could lead the revolution that Israel needed so desperately. The people would follow. Rome could be thrown off.

As Judas spent more and more time with Jesus it is not hard to imagine his expectations growing. He listened to the teaching, watched the healing power touch the lives of people. This man had power over the waves of the sea and the boundaries of death. Here was a man of God, the man of God who could raise up the nation of Israel. As the relationship between Jesus and Judas developed in trust, Judas became the treasurer of the band of disciples, taking care of the daily needs of the little community — staying in close to the man who would fulfil his expectations.

Ray Anderson, a friend of mine, wrote a disturbing little book a few years back called *The Gospel According to Judas*. In this thought-provoking theological reflection on Judas, Ray creates a dialogue between Jesus and Judas that continues after the resurrection. You may not agree with all of Anderson's conclusions or suggestions, but I commend the book as a mind stretching and faith enriching essay.

According to Anderson, Judas' betrayal of Jesus is an act of love. Starting from the assumption that only love can be betrayed, Anderson unfolds the relationship between Judas and Jesus in line with Judas' expectations that Jesus would in fact be the spark that ignited Israel against Rome. The more time Judas spent with Jesus, the stronger the bond of love and brotherhood developed until Judas feared that his own agenda for Israel would be swallowed up in Jesus' intention to walk right into the hands of the Jewish leaders. A personal relationship and a personal agenda — now in conflict. This man that he loved and followed was not going to lead the insurrection by himself! Judas had to choose: to pursue his personal commitments or to allow God to set the path through Jesus. . . . In the end his own agenda dominated and he decided to force Jesus' hand.

Perutz was right. Judas did not betray Jesus to the Jewish leaders. The soldiers did not need Judas to point out who Jesus was. Any number of persons could have made the identification. He betrayed the love that bound him to Jesus. He allowed his pride to take over, his personal agenda to take priority and set aside his love for Jesus and his love by Jesus. Judas probably believed that if he could provoke the authorities into arresting Jesus, the crowds would raise up in his defense and the revolution would begin.

Judas did not want to have Jesus killed. He *wanted* Peter to go for his sword. He wanted them all to go for their swords and for the fight to begin! But he had been too caught up with his personal agenda to understand that Jesus would not fight, that God had a different plan in mind. When he finally realized that rather than starting the revolution, he had succeeded in participating in the death of this person who had loved him so deeply, Judas was crushed. Like Peter he is humiliated by his own weakness and failure. Like Peter he had betrayed the love of his Lord. But unlike Peter, his betrayal filled him with such despair that he took his own life. Burdened by responsibility for the results of his action, he confesses his sin, throws away the money and hangs himself. He had failed to achieve the personal agenda that he brought to his relationship with Jesus, and in the process had precipitated the death of the one whom he had followed these three years as the fulfillment of all of his expectations. A tragic figure. A man torn between his personal agenda for life and his desire to follow Jesus. A person with great expectations for God but not truly open to God's plans for his life.

Now, of all the characters I could have picked to look at on the first chapel of a new year at Regent, why Judas? Maybe it's because I see a little of Judas in me and it scares me. Maybe it's because I am afraid of that little bit of Judas that resides in any group of people starting a new phase of their walk with God.

We begin a new year together this week. We are a community of men and women collected by God from all over the world to be a studying, learning, teaching community in Vancouver this year. Each one of us begins this year with fresh expectations. We expect to meet God. We expect to learn something. We expect to be equipped to integrate our faith with our lives and our work. We expect to be trained as leaders for the church, as ministers for the marketplace. We all have high expectations for this year!

We have rearranged our lives, saved our money, moved, in some cases, literally around the world. We have plans for God. Like Judas, we have great expectations!

Last year I was teaching in Chicago. A staff member at the school invited me to dinner with several of the students at the seminary. As we sat around the table talking after dinner, one student stopped the conversation by announcing that he had a question he wanted me to address. Everyone was quiet as he put out his question in a slightly aggressive manner. He said: "I was born on the south side of Chicago. At my age, I am supposed to be on drugs, in jail or dead. But I believe that God wants me to do something great with my life. I don't have the advantage of being a white middle-class male like you, but I want to do something great with my life like you have. How can I be sure I do it?" I had been enjoying the evening up to that point!

My answer was not deeply theological but it was personal. He was asking about something I had thought about — my expectations. Looking back, I guess my answer was basically a suggestion that he rethink his expectations.

I identified with his feeling that God has something great for him to do. I told him I had had that sense from the time I was a little boy and was sure that many others have as well. I have always believed that God has something important for me to do with my life. The problem is . . . *I don't know if I have already done it, if I am doing it now or if it is still ahead of me!* The only thing I can do is be faithful to what I have been called to do today and trust God to decide what is important. Perhaps the only appropriate response to expectation is faithfulness. The rest is up to God.

It was also a surprise for him and for me to deal with his other expectation — that skin color and economic upbringing will necessarily shape what God can do with us. When I inquired further, I learned that all of his siblings had grown up in South Chicago, had completed college, had not done drugs, been in jail or died. He was shocked to learn that that very year my younger brother had been violently murdered in California. A Chicago ghetto or a San

Diego suburb may shape our expectations, but they do not determine what God will do.

Expectations. We want so much from God, or perhaps so little! But our expectations can severely blind us to what God is actually doing in our midst. It is not what we think will happen or what we believe should happen. It is what God does with us that counts.

At the beginning of a new year together we gather in community to encourage one another in our walk with God. As we arrive in Vancouver with a heart to know God and great expectations for what he will do this year, it is appropriate to remember Judas, a man of great expectations, who let his expectations blind him to what God was doing before his eyes.

God will meet you this year but it may take a very different form than you have been expecting. You are here for a reason, but you may not be the best judge of that reason. Set your expectations for God aside — and listen for God's expectations for you. Invest yourself faithfully in this community this year, in your studies, in one another. Pursue your walk with God — and trust that his expectations will be fulfilled.

Like the disciples in the painting of *The Last Supper*, we sit at the table with Jesus this year. Together we will learn from him. Together we will explore what God is saying to the world, to the church, to Regent and to each of us as we move into a new year. When this year is completed, may the painter say, "There is a face that is open to God!"

Regent Chapel
September 14, 1993

14

Living Proof

*S*ix days before the Passover, Jesus arrived at Bethany, where Lazarus lived, whom Jesus had raised from the dead. Here a dinner was given in Jesus' honor. Martha served, while Lazarus was among those reclining at the table with him. Then Mary took about a pint of pure nard, an expensive perfume; she poured it on Jesus' feet and wiped his feet with her hair. And the house was filled with the fragrance of the perfume.

But one of his disciples, Judas Iscariot, who was later to betray him, objected, "Why wasn't this perfume sold and the money given to the poor? It was worth a year's wages." He did not say this because he cared about the poor but because he was a thief; as keeper of the money bag, he used to help himself to what was put into it.

"Leave her alone," Jesus replied. "It was intended that she should save this perfume for the day of my burial. You will always have the poor among you, but you will not always have me."

> *Meanwhile a large crowd of Jews found out that Jesus was there and came, not only because of him but also to see Lazarus, whom he had raised from the dead. So the chief priests made plans to kill Lazarus as well, for on account of him many of the Jews were going over to Jesus and putting their faith in him.*
>
> John 12:1-11

It's a Saturday night. Friends have gathered to celebrate. These have been emotional days. In fact the past few years have been rather exciting and unusual — ever since Jesus went to the wedding in Cana and began to demonstrate the power of God through his miracles and teaching. Jesus has clearly stirred things up. Life will never be the same. But this last week has left everyone emotionally drained. Lazarus! Lazarus died . . . but now he lives!

We don't know much about Lazarus except that he was the brother of Mary and Martha — a friend of Jesus. A week ago, however, Lazarus was dying. His sisters were overwhelmed with fear for his life and sent for Jesus in the desperate hope that he might come in time and heal Lazarus as he had healed others over these past few years. But Jesus did not come. And Lazarus died.

And we know the story. Lazarus was buried and sealed in the tomb. Outside the family and friends mourned his death, probably a little hurt and angry that Jesus had not intervened and saved his friend. Then four days after his death, Jesus did arrive and to the astonishment of the mourners, he raised Lazarus from the tomb, back to life. The whole town is talking about it. Lazarus has been resurrected! Emotions pouring out in grief have been jerked into reverse, erupting in joy. Everyone is celebrating this wonderful news. Lazarus has been resurrected.

In our text this morning, we walk into one of these celebrations. A Saturday night dinner party at the home of Mary, Martha and Lazarus. The meal is spread out on the table. The guests are reclining around the table. There is probably a fire in the hearth accenting the warmth and joy felt by everyone in the room. John describes the familiar scene for us, sketching some of the characters present. Jesus — the guest of honour. Lazarus reclining at the banquet table with him. Martha busy as usual serving up the meal; Mary washing Jesus' feet with perfume; Judas complaining about the waste of money; the religious leaders plotting to kill Lazarus.

This is a party thrown in honor of Jesus — their friend who had indeed arrived at their time of deepest need and sorrow — who had reversed what they thought irreversible. Jesus, who had given Lazarus new life is being celebrated at this party thrown by his grateful friends. What a party! A celebration of resurrection! Can you imagine a happier scene? Pain erased by joy. Tears replaced by laughter. Grief dismissed by gratitude. A room full of people bubbling over with emotion as they celebrate the resurrection of Lazarus.

I find it instructive to note the various responses to the resurrection that are reflected in the characters sketched in this scene. Each one faces this unimaginable reality and responds in their own way. At this dinner celebration, as friends gather to honor Jesus and share their joy, we can see four distinct responses to the resurrection.

The response of service

Martha responds with *service*. She immediately plans a banquet and throws herself into busy service for her Lord. She prepares a feast, with the rich aromas of food cooking, flowing through the house. She is the hostess, finding fulfilment in lavishing hospitality upon her guests. Most of the pictures we have of Martha in the New Testament leave me feeling tired! She is busy — always busy — always engaged in service, helping, caring, working. In many ways Martha is the quintessential Christian worker, selflessly engaged in constant and continuous ministry to those around her, and as we know from Luke 10, not always understanding why everyone else is not as committed to service as she is.

The response of worship

Mary responds with *worship*, giving of her resources and herself as she washes Jesus' feet, drying them with her long hair. As Martha finds fulfillment in active ministry, Mary seeks her satisfaction in reflective devotion. Mary takes a very expensive bottle of perfume — worth a year's annual salary — rubs the fragrant oil into the feet of Jesus and wipes them dry with her long, dark hair. An act of generous and selfless devotion that does not go unnoticed.

How could it? Not only does one of the owners of the house take on the posture of a servant, but the pungent odors of the perfume waft through the air competing with the smells of cooking, overpowering the senses of all present around the table. Mary represents the pure pietist in this story, responding to the resurrection with generous and lavish worship pointing everyone present to Jesus, her Lord.

Service and piety — the two most basic responses to resurrection are incarnated in the two sisters of Lazarus — Martha and Mary. Luke (chapter 10) tells us that both of these responses are valid and necessary to keep in balance. Service without worship does not point to God; worship without service is not productive faith. Service and piety — two responses to the resurrection of Lazarus.

The response of the activist

Judas, however, offers a third response. He gets angry. He neither serves nor worships. As one of Jesus' disciples, we are not surprised to find him dining at the feast. He has been with Jesus throughout his public ministry. He had watched with surprise as Jesus delayed responding to Mary and Martha's call for help. He had watched with pain as Jesus grieved the death of Lazarus. He had joined with resignation the little band that accompanied Jesus to Bethany expecting that this would provoke the authorities. And he had watched with amazement when Jesus brought Lazarus back to life. Judas is an *activist*. He is a zealot who longs for revolution, for the uprising that will free Israel from the occupation of the Romans. He likes the power that he sees manifested by Jesus, but he wants it channeled into his own vision for Israel. He too has seen Lazarus come forth, yet Mary's act of devotion blocks his understanding of the resurrection. He is the administrator of the band of disciples responsible for the funds. As he watches Mary lavishly use wealth to wash feet, he responds with anger. With one eye toward the revolution that he hopes Jesus will lead and another eye to his own personal agenda, which John tells us he tends to fund from the contributions to Jesus' ministry, Judas allows his personal agenda to blind him to the significance of the resurrection. He wants to get things moving. He doesn't have time for banquets and hero worship. There is a revolution to fight! He knows what he wants from God, and he wants to get on with it. This resurrection has been a frustrating diversion from an activist's carefully planned itinerary.

Lazarus

Three responses to the resurrection: service, piety, activism. But there is a fourth person identified at the table with Jesus: Lazarus.

What about Lazarus? What does he do? Nothing! *Lazarus just lies there and eats!* He is not serving — working actively for God. He is not worshipping, at least in any visible active way. He is not worrying about finances or personal agendas. He is simply eating dinner, enjoying himself and luxuriating in the fact that he is alive. Last week he was dying — no hope, only sorrow and death. Now he's alive and eating with Jesus, his friend. Just relaxing. He used to be dead! Now he's alive. And he is enjoying life.

The Religious Leaders

Four responses to the resurrection. But notice whom the Jewish leaders want to kill! Not Martha, the consummate Christian minister and servant; not Mary, the passionate leader of worship; not Judas, the religious activist. They want to kill Lazarus! Why?

Because Lazarus' very *life* is a testimony to the power of God present in Jesus. He didn't need to *do* anything. He *was*. He was a product, a prototype if you will, of the resurrected life. He had new life and it was obvious to those who knew him. That was enough to draw people to God. And that is what terrified the religious leaders who preferred to have people satisfy their need for God through the normal channels of organized religion — a system they controlled.

Lazarus is relaxing and eating. Yet he is the threat. He is living the resurrected life. He is not busy working, not busy worshipping, not busy organizing. He is simply *living* before God and people as one who enjoys the resurrection life — living proof of the resurrection.

What about us?

What about us? We live on the other side of resurrection. We affirm the new life empowered by the resurrection spirit of God. How do we respond to this resurrection? Are we busy in service and worship and Christian activism — worthy responses — but maybe not a threat? Or are we modern day Lazarus' enjoying the feast with such gusto that it is obvious something has happened? Do our very lives, our daily existence, remind people that Jesus is alive and God is at work? Are we products of the resurrection whose daily lives testify to the power of God and point people to the presence of Christ?

This is a point of tension for most of us. We believe that we have been resurrected in Christ, but we still live as though we have to prove something. I trust God but am still entombed by my own fears and need for approval. Faculty are tempted to find their worth in their writing or public speaking. Students look to grades and job offers. Why is it so hard to relax like Lazarus?

We have just celebrated another Easter — affirmed the truth of resurrection: Christ has done it all. And again, I needed the reminder — again, I needed to be called free from all that entombs me. As I celebrated Easter, thinking about this talk, I wondered: what is my tomb? What dark, deep sealed hole do I need to be freed from?

Like Lazarus, I know that I have a new life in Christ. I know that nothing I can do can negate what God has done for me in the resurrection. Resurrection life is mine to live. And yet I struggle with fears; I am afraid of failure. I want to be perceived as a good teacher, a good administrator. I succumb to my needs for control. I still work hard to achieve a validation and recognition that pales beside the call: Lazarus come forth.

Why do we struggle to perform for God? Why do we need one another's validation and the affirmation of our ministry so strongly? Why do we strive to be Marys, Marthas, Judases, and even religious leaders, instead of lying back and enjoying the feast. I want to be like Lazarus!

It's easy for me to find my Mary and my Martha, even my Judas. But hard to find my Lazarus. I can respond comfortably with service, worship and action. But it is hard to relax in the security of what God has already done. Easter is an annual reminder to *let my Lazarus loose* — accept forgiveness, accept who I am and enjoy the life that I have been given. There is nothing I need to do. God has done it all. It is God's work in Christ that changes this world. Not mine.

You have just spent a year or more at Regent College. Faculty, staff and friends have shared in your theological education. According to our catalog, you have been "equipped to live and work as mature leaders in this world." If you have learned to lead out as servants, caring for the needs of the men and women that God will send across your path, then you will make a difference in people's lives. If you have learned to lead out in worship, pointing the people around you to God, then you will make a difference in the church. If you have learned how to lead out as leaders of the organized mission of the church, challenging the claims of our culture, you will make a difference in this world. But if that is all that you are, it may not be enough.

The world needs Lazaruses — people who have experienced the resurrection life — people who find their identity, their security, their meaning in relationship with God in Jesus Christ — living proof. Service, piety and activism are not substitutes for living in relationship with God. That is what they saw in Lazarus. That is what they must see in us.

The world is watching. They note our busyness about Christian service. They observe our stated piety and acts of worship. They look at our organizations and missions. What they really want to know is have we found that deep security and joy in our relationship with God or is all this activity part of our frantic attempts to find worth and value. And we all know how easy it is for us to find our identity in one of these roles.

We do not know what Lazarus did for a living or for a ministry. Lazarus died. Now he lives. That's really all we know about Lazarus. But that's enough. We know Lazarus as one for whom God acted — not for his service, his piety, his leadership. He was a miracle — a new man — literally. He didn't need to do anything to point to God. And that I believe is the message of Lazarus as we come to the end of another academic year, standing on this side of the resurrection. As we prepare to go out into a variety of activities around the world, Lazarus reminds us that *it is the work of God that is life changing, not the ministries of men and women.*

You go out from Regent College to serve, to worship, to lead. May you hear also the words of Jesus: Lazarus (your name) come forth, and remember to find your life and meaning in what God has done not in what you are doing. May you live and enjoy your resurrection life with such gusto that people know that God is at work.

Regent Chapel
April 19, 1994

15

Coming Together

*P*aul and Timothy, servants of Christ
Jesus, To all the saints in Christ Jesus
at Philippi, together with the overseers
and deacons:

*Grace and peace to you from God our Father and the
Lord Jesus Christ.*

*I thank my God every time I remember you. In all
my prayers for all of you, I always pray with joy because of
your partnership in the gospel from the first day until now,
being confident of this, that he who began a good work in
you will carry it on to completion until the day of Christ
Jesus.*

*It is right for me to feel this way about all of you,
since I have you in my heart; for whether I am in chains
or defending and confirming the gospel, all of you share in
God's grace with me. God can testify how I long for all of
you with the affection of Christ Jesus.*

And this is my prayer: that your love may abound

*more and more in knowledge and depth of insight, so that
you may be able to discern what is best and may be pure
and blameless until the day of Christ, filled with the fruit
of righteousness that comes through Jesus Christ — to the
glory and praise of God.*

Philippians 1:1-11

A new year — a new community coming together to worship and study for these next months. We sit here in relative comfort on padded seats, with the knowledge that lunch is being prepared for us right outside our doors. But we read this morning a letter from a prisoner. What can a nearly 2000-year-old letter from prison teach us about the journey of theological education that we are about to undertake together this year?

I'm a little sensitive about 2000-year-old things these days. . . . In June, Edwin Hui and I joined Barry Hawes and Jon Scott, two members of the Board of Governors of Regent College, on a visit to Singapore, Kuala Lumpur and Hong Kong to visit alumni and talk to theological schools in the three countries. I wanted to bring Beverly back something she would value. Beverly is a potter and likes old asian pottery. In a back road of Hong Kong, I found a beautiful old clay pot, which the antiquities dealer claimed was made about the same time that Paul wrote this letter to Philippi. It was quite a find. However, when I showed it to Edwin, he immediately started talking to a member of the hotel staff in Cantonese and they were laughing. That was my first hint. When I returned to Vancouver and presented the gift to Beverly, she was very gracious and appreciative, but illustrated from the piece of pottery that we were probably not talking about 2000 years . . . more like 2000 days! And if that isn't bad enough, people visiting our home this summer have regularly asked if Beverly made it! So much for my archeological skills!

But the letter we have just read from is indeed nearly 2000 years old. And yet it offers, I believe, some timeless truth that applies directly to our task of theological education.

As Paul sits in Rome under house arrest, he writes to the Christians in Philippi with several things on his mind, not the least of which is his own fate as he awaits trial and final judgement from the Roman authorities. He wants to express his appreciation for the Philippian Christians' financial support; but he also is concerned by signs of disunity within the community. Members of the community are bickering, more worried about themselves than the community. They are not keeping their minds focused on Christ, but rather have been distracted by their personal agendas. He comments on these concerns from the perspective of his own situation. While he is not talking about theological education per se, he is talking about the Christian life with principles that I believe are applicable to our year together.

This morning I would like to comment on four points related to theological education that I think Paul is underlining in this opening to his letter:

1. Theological education is a partnership.
2. Theological education is a journey with God.
3. In theological education, knowledge is penultimate to character.
4. Christian character always points to God.

Theological education is a partnership

Paul is sitting in prison in Rome reflecting on his life and ministry and reviewing some of the things for which he is thankful. He has had a long and successful ministry and now awaits trial before the Roman court. His outcome is not certain. Death is a possibility that lurks like a shadow in the corner of his room — a possibility that casts its perspective on his thinking.

Paul is writing to the Philippians to say thank you, expressing his appreciation for their financial investment in his ministry. They are partners with him in his preaching and church planting ministry and share even now in his sustenance during his imprisonment. Basically this is a fund raising letter, or more precisely, a follow-up thank you letter encouraging their stewardship and the corollary growth in their own walk with God.

I can understand a little of what Paul felt. Not the prison part, but the thank you letter. This summer Doug Bennett, our Chief Development Officer, and I wrote over 1000 thank you letters to the partners of Regent College — the men and women who invest so generously in our mission as a College. They are indeed partners, sharing personally in your education this year.

A friend and philanthropist, C. Davis Weyerhaeuser, once said that God had given him the gifts of creating wealth and stewardship. Everything he touches turns to gold. But when he invests that wealth in a church, he becomes a preacher; when he invests it in a seminary, he becomes a theologian; when he invests it in Young Life, he becomes a youth minister. He becomes a partner matching his gifts with the persons he is funding.

As you sit here in this chapel, nearly 1000 partners in your education are praying for you and working today to earn the funds that they will contribute this year to make your education possible.

I know having just paid your tuition, you feel like a pretty big investor yourself, and you are! But the total cost for educating each full-time student at Regent this year will be over $10,000. Your tuition is as low as it is because someone out there is working today to pay the rest of it for you. That's partnership — and that's what Paul is writing about — the people whom God raises up to join with you in your education and ministry through their financial partnership. He is expressing his thanks as we do here at Regent — demonstrating again that the act of saying thank you is an acknowledgement of our dependence — on the partners and on God. Remember those people who are standing with you financially. Pray for our partners as they pray for you.

Partners in ministry. . . . But there is another side to this idea of partnership. We are partners together in the gospel — in our walk with Christ — in our theological education if you will.

When I welcomed the new students last week, I noted that you join this community reshaping it with the gifts that you bring. We are in this together. You come to learn, but you also have something to teach. We need to avoid the traditional educational model of ignorant students sitting at the feet of learned scholars. Most of you are not ignorant students. Many of you come with years of Christian maturity and ministry, years of vocational integration, already making significant contributions in your own career. And those of us on the faculty and staff also represent a spectrum of age, experience and maturity. And those with the most age, experience and maturity are usually the first to confess that they have so much more to learn. We are at best learning associates — partners on the journey of theological education. We will learn together and we will learn from each other.

In Southeast Asia this summer, I was humbled again by the level of responsibility that our alumni hold in the various cities that we visited, responsibilities that many of them had before they came to Regent College. I was reminded articulately that we do not always draw on the strengths of those that God sends into this community. One prominent professor commented that while she was on sabbatical leave at Regent, we tended to treat her as a student rather than a colleague with experience and ideas about integration.

We are a community represented and defined by our diversity. Seeing Regent's ministry to the Pacific Rim through the eyes of our alumni reminded me that we have much to learn from each other and only together do we form the community of Christ's body.

Paul understood this. He saw himself in partnership with his churches. I believe that even as Paul writes to the Church in Philippi, he is writing also to himself, working out his own faith in the face of tensions he feels about his own calling and experience of community.

We are partners together — faculty, staff, students, board, investors — associates learning together and from one another. May we be receptive learners and willing teachers as this year unfolds.

Theological Education is a journey with God

But theological education is more than partnership between the members of this community. It is also partnership with God. Even as Paul thanks the Philippians for their partnership with him in his ministry and underlines how it will add to their own growth and maturity, he reminds them that it is God who is at work in them and who will continue to work until their completion at the return of Christ.

Your time of study at Regent College is not your theological education. We are only one segment in a much longer journey — a journey you set out upon when you first encountered God in Christ. Those of us who spend our lives in theological education know only too well that when you receive your degrees and diplomas and leave this community your theological education is not over. Convocation does not confer maturity or completion of your journey. It is simply the transition point where passengers in transit move from one segment of their journey to another.

This summer, as part of my continued Canadianization, I read about the exploratory journeys of George Vancouver, Alexander Mackenzie, Simon Fraser and David Thompson as attempts were made to define a route between the Atlantic and Pacific coasts of Canada. Each explorer scouted one segment of the journey through British Columbia — one piece for which history remembers them. A small piece of the full trading route and a small portion of the total number of miles in their journeys. They worked long and hard; they learned and they shared what they knew. Together they made accessible a beautiful new country.

This time at Regent College is one segment of your journey with God. Each of us enters this communal segment at a different stage in our own journey. We have been brought together to learn from each other and we have much to teach each other as we walk side by side. Paul wants us to recognize that we are partners on the journey, but even more to remember that it is a journey with God that we are about. It is God who brought each one of us to Regent College. I find this an awesome and humbling thought! And it is God who is preparing each one of us for the next segment of our journey with him. May this year be one in which God continues to shape you into the maturity and character of Christ.

And that brings me to my third point.

In theological education, knowledge is penultimate to character

In his prayer for the Philippian Christians, Paul asks that they may be overflowing with love — a love that is directed by knowledge and understanding, by intellectual and moral insight — a love that is manifested in the fruit of righteousness — that fruit of the spirit that marks Christian character. Paul prays for knowledge and insight but not just for intellectual growth. He wants a knowledge that is so integrated with love and discernment that it produces a life of character that reflects the presence of Jesus Christ.

In theological education study should produce character

In a recent issue of *TIME* magazine, the editors were lamenting the loss of character in North America. Focusing primarily on the political campaign in the U.S. and the "character" challenge of Ross Perot, they expressed concern in the lack of honesty, integrity and vision in public officials and private citizens. They were not very clear what character is, but they were convinced that we had lost it.

Theological education is about character. It is a process of theological and biblical study intended to bring you into the presence of God, to equip you with the tools and desire to pursue the mind of Christ. It is a journey with God intended to grow you in spiritual maturity, to fill you with such things as compassion, kindness, humility, gentleness, patience, forgiveness, love and unity. The diploma of graduation from this program is not frameable for your wall. It is worn in your character for the world to see. What we are about together this year is a study of theology that will construct a world view out of which we can live in this world and shape a personal and community character that will reflect the presence of Christ whereever we go in this world.

At some point in your study at Regent you should read *Pia Desideria*, by Philip Jacob Spener, the Father of German pietism. Spener, like Paul, was disappointed with the state of the Church around him and tended to blame the theological schools for their contribution to the problem. In this little book, he attacks those who thrive on intellectual pursuits and clever theological debates without living a life of holiness. He writes in 1675:

> It becomes apparent that disputing is not enough either to maintain the truth among ourselves or to impart it to the erring. The holy love of God is necessary. If only we Evangelicals would make it our serious business to offer God the fruits of his truth in fervent love, conduct ourselves in a manner worthy of our calling, and show this in recognizable and unalloyed love of our neighbours, including those who are heretics . . .
> (*Pia Desideria,* p. 102)

Regarding students he says: "Besides, students should unceasingly have it impressed upon them that holy life is not of less consequence than diligence and study, indeed that study without piety is worthless" (Pia Disideria, p. 104).

He is no less articulate about the role of theological faculty:

> The professors could themselves accomplish a great deal here by their example . . . if they would conduct themselves as men (and women) who have died unto the world, in everything would seek not their own glory, gain or pleasure but rather the glory of their God and the salvation of those entrusted to them, and

would accommodate all their studies, writing of books, lessons, lectures, disputations, and other activities to this end.

(*Pia Disideria*, p. 104)

Spener's passion for an approach to theological education that blended piety with intellectual study flows out of his deep commitment to lay ministry. Over 330 years ago he was encouraging the laity and the clergy to recognize and encourage the gifted members of the congregation to bring about the needed reform in the church. Philip Spener was "very Regent College" and I commend his book to your attention.

This year the Strategic Planning Committee of the Board at Regent will be looking again at this question of character as it applies to our community together. What are those values and beliefs that shape our life together and how are they worked out in our unique blend of organization and community. We talk much about community and character. We want to be sure that we live and behave what we teach — that our voice and our touch come together.

Max DePree has been a friend and mentor of mine for years. In his little book, *Leadership Jazz*, he opens with a story about voice and touch that illustrate their intimate connection:

> Esther, my wife, and I have a granddaughter named Zoe, the Greek word for "life." She was born prematurely and weighed one pound, seven ounces, so small that my wedding ring could slide up her arm to her shoulder. The neonatologist who first examined her told us that she had a 5 to 10 percent chance of living three days. When Esther and I scrubbed up for our first visit and saw Zoe in her isolette in the neonatal intensive care unit, she had two IVs in her navel, one in her foot, a monitor on each side of her chest, and a respirator tube and a feeding tube in her mouth.
>
> To complicate matters, Zoe's biological father had jumped ship the month before Zoe was born. Realizing this, a wise and caring nurse named Ruth gave me my instructions. "For the next several months, at least, you're the surrogate father. I want you to come to the

hospital every day to visit Zoe, and when you come, I would like you to rub her body and her legs and arms with the tip of your finger. While you're caressing her, you should tell her over and over how much you love her, because she has to be able to connect your voice to your touch."

Ruth was doing exactly the right thing on Zoe's behalf (and, of course, on my behalf as well), and without realizing it she was giving me one of the best possible descriptions of the work of a leader. At the core of becoming a leader is the need always to connect one's voice and one's touch.

(*Leadership Jazz*, p. 1-3)

At Regent College we want our voice and our touch to be connected. And we pray that your experience of theological education this year will make that connection for you. May your knowledge gained shape your love in a way that takes root in your soul, producing a life of Christ-like character that points people directly to God. May your voice always be connected to your touch.

There is one final point that we need to note — the point with which Paul concludes this section of his letter.

Christian character always points to God

This is the goal of theological education — an intellectually formed Christ-like character that points people directly to God — a life lived "to the glory and praise of God." This is what our partnership is about. As we share this year together, as we study, learn and teach together, as we grow in Christ-like maturity and increase in the reflection of the fruit of his spirit it should result in the praise of God.

This summer we interviewed a world class scholar about a position at Regent. We told him that his reputation was helpful, his scholarship and publications a sign of his theological competence, but we wanted to know about his character — only that can tell us whether his theology has taken root. Does it point to a great scholar? Or does it point to God?

This will be the true test of your theological education at Regent College.

To whose glory are you undertaking this journey? To whose glory are we partners together in this community? May all that we say and do, individually and corporately, point one another and those outside our community to Jesus Christ. May this be a year in which God is praised by us and because of us.

Regent Chapel
September 15, 1992

16

The Last Lecture

*F*inally, my brothers and sisters, rejoice in the Lord! It is no trouble for me to write the same things to you again, and it is a safeguard for you.

Watch out for those dogs, those persons who do evil, those mutilators of the flesh. For it is we who are the circumcision, we who worship by the Spirit of God, who glory in Christ Jesus, and who put no confidence in the flesh — though I myself have reasons for such confidence.

If others think they have reasons to put confidence in the flesh, I have more: circumcised on the eighth day, of the people of Israel, of the tribe of Benjamin, a Hebrew of Hebrews; in regard to the law, a Pharisee; as for zeal, persecuting the church; as for legalistic righteousness, faultless.

But whatever was to my profit I now consider loss for the sake of Christ. What is more, I consider everything a loss compared to the surpassing greatness of knowing Christ Jesus my Lord, for whose sake I have lost all things. I consider them rubbish, that I may gain Christ and be found in him, not having a righteousness of my own that comes from the law, but that which is through faith in Christ

*— the righteousness that comes from God and is by faith.
I want to know Christ and the power of his resurrection
and the fellowship of sharing in his sufferings, becoming
like him in his death, and so, somehow, to attain to the
resurrection from the dead.*

*Not that I have already obtained all this, or have
already been made perfect, but I press on to take hold of
that for which Christ Jesus took hold of me. Brothers and
sisters, I do not consider myself yet to have taken hold of it.
But one thing I do: Forgetting what is behind and strain-
ing toward what is ahead, I press on toward the goal to
win the prize for which God has called me heavenward
in Christ Jesus.*

*All of us who are mature should take such a view of
things. And if on some point you think differently, that too
God will make clear to you. Only let us live up to what we
have already attained.*

*Join with others in following my example, friends,
and take note of those who live according to the pattern
we gave you. For, as I have often told you before and
now say again, even with tears, many live as enemies of
the cross of Christ. Their destiny is destruction, their god
is their stomach, and their glory is in their shame. Their
mind is on earthly things. But our citizenship is in heaven.
And we eagerly await a Saviour from there, the Lord
Jesus Christ, who, by the power that enables him to bring
everything under his control, will transform our lowly bodies so that they will be like his glorious body.*

*Therefore, my brothers and sisters, you whom I love
and long for, my joy and crown, that is how you should
stand firm in the Lord, dear friends.!*

*I plead with Euodia and I plead with Syntyche to
agree with each other in the Lord. Yes, and I ask you, true
companion, help these women who have contended at my
side in the cause of the gospel, along with Clement and the
rest of my fellow workers, whose names are in the book of
life.*

Rejoice in the Lord always. I will say it again: Rejoice!
Let your gentleness be evident to all. The Lord is near.
Do not be anxious about anything, but in everything,
by prayer and petition, with thanksgiving, present your
requests to God. And the peace of God, which transcends
all understanding, will guard your hearts and your minds
in Christ Jesus

Finally, brothers and sisters, whatever is true, what-
ever is noble, whatever is right, whatever is pure, whatever
is lovely, whatever is admirable—if anything is excellent or
praiseworthy—think about such things. Whatever you
have learned or received or heard from me, or seen in me
—put it into practice. And the God of peace will be with
you.

Philippians 3:1-4:9

What do you say when it's time to say goodbye? When a community that has worshipped and studied together for the past year comes to the end of its shared journey? What final words of wisdom do you leave lingering in the air, hoping they will continue to whisper over the shoulders of friends moving off in various directions?

The Apostle Paul has been sitting in Rome under house arrest writing a letter to his friends in Philippi. He started this letter intentionally to say thanks. To express his appreciation to the Church in Philippi for their financial support and prayers for his ministry. He is grateful for their encouragement and partnership as he awaits the outcome of his trial — the final judgement on his future.

With his own future ambiguous, he does not know whether he will see them or write them again. So he throws in a little advice and instruction. He has heard of some tensions within the church and writes to them about their partnership in community, about their journey with God and about personal character modeled after Christ.

As he moves toward the close of his letter, knowing that this could be the last words that he will be able to communicate to them, I can imagine Paul pondering carefully his conclusion. The last two chapters of this letter feel like the last lecture in Paul's notes for the Philippians. The final instructions before he sends the letter off.

Each faculty member here can identify with this, as can I, in this last chapel of the year. A last shot — a final word — the last piece of advice. What are those final words that we want to leave with you that capture what we have been teaching in class all term — that summarize what we hope you will take away from your time at Regent College.

As Paul sits there and ponders his concluding thoughts, he could well have been a member of this community because his final words of advice fit very well the end of an academic year. I can imagine Paul here today sending you out with four final instructions in his closing lecture.

1. Don't rest on your education.
2. Resist legalism.
3. Focus on your walk with Christ.
4. Your character is your true diploma.

Don't rest on your education

In three weeks over 150 of you will process into Convocation to receive your diplomas and degrees. This piece of parchment symbolizes the completion of a serious program of study. You have worked hard . . . long hours in the library . . . cramped hands from taking notes . . . sore fingers from typing papers . . . tired eyes from reading thousands of pages. You have worked hard. You have earned this diploma and you deserve the celebration that we will share together.

In full pomp and circumstance we will parade around in our academic regalia, announcing to the world that another group of men and women have mastered or "DIPped-into" the disciplines of biblical study and theological thinking. We will announce awards of achievement and place hoods of distinction upon many of your shoulders. It will be a glorious evening — an enjoyable celebration of the Regent community.   You have finished your education!

Not quite! I don't want to spoil your party by reminding you of the obvious — but you're not done. You have only reached another fork on the road, another jog on your journey of life and growth. You have completed one portion of your journey that we shared together, but you cannot stop now. Your journey is not over.

I think this is what Paul has in mind. He recounts his accomplishments as a Jew — all his education and training — and wipes them away as inconsequential compared to his relationship with Christ. Even as he seeks to grow in his knowledge of God and become Christ-like in his life as he sits there in prison, he realizes that he must constantly forget what he has accomplished and press on to what is ahead as he follows God's calling heavenward. His journey is not over . . . and it only moves forward.

This reminds me of one of the canoe trips I took with my friend Don Bosch. Don and I have been canoeing white water rivers in California annually for the past seven years. The first years we learned a lot the hard way, spilling ourselves and our gear into the river many times through inexperience and dumb mistakes. But we learned. Each year we improved. We read books on canoeing, we watched videos, we practiced. We studied the rapids before we entered them and learned how to plan a strategy that would see us through without capsizing.

It was our third year on the Trinity River in northern California. We were in the middle of a 40-mile stretch and had come to a cascading rapid that we had walked around in previous years. We stood on a cliff above the rapids and studied the river. The river dropped through a roiling cascade about 200 feet directly towards a wall of rock. As the water rushed against the rock, it surged backwards, pushing the currant sharply to the left downstream and around another bend. We thought we had learned enough to try it. We planned our strategy and returned to the river.

Placing the bow of the canoe into the top of the cascade, we plunged down toward the rock wall, Don steering in the stern, while I used a bracing stroke to keep the bow up out of the waves. Just as we touched the water surging back from the rock, we executed a text book perfect cross-draw stroke and turned neatly into the current, rushing past the rock wall and floating comfortably down the river.

We were ecstatic. Everything we had learned and planned had worked flawlessly. All of our study and practice had paid off. We knew how to do it. We cheered and rehearsed the perfection of our manoeuvre, relaxing as our adrenalin returned to normal — oblivious to the fact that we were still floating rapidly downstream!

Suddenly we noticed two rocks directly in the middle of the river. Without time to plan we sat up quickly and steered between the rocks. I have vividly etched in my memory a pure green tongue of water that converged between those rocks as we slid out over a two foot drop we had not seen. Don says my last words were "We don't do this!" as the bow of the canoe plunged down and I went flying over the front of the canoe into the cold river.

We still talk about that trip. The green tongue has become part of the folklore of our canoeing group. We learned clearly that on the river you cannot rest on your accomplishments. One eye must be looking ahead and planning or the green tongue will swallow you!

Your journey also is not over. Everything you have studied, that we have taught and learned together, must now be rooted and built upon, invested and developed, applied and adjusted. The journey continues. What for you is the conclusion of an academic program, for the faculty represents one of our most disturbing realities. We haven't given you enough, yet we may have given you too much!

Every faculty committee that sits down to design a curriculum gets up from the table frustrated. There is so much to learn, so much to teach. How can we possibly package what we believe is important into one, two or even three years? When we design a degree program we know how much we have left out and it leaves us uncomfortable. We know that we can only start you on a lifetime of study, point in a few directions and seek to stir up your interest to explore further on your own. We know that we can talk about theology, integration, spirituality and ministry in the classroom, but until you have worked it out in the reality of daily life it can't really take root. We send you out from Convocation knowing that we have fed you hor'd'ourvres and shown you the menu, and praying that we have given you an appetite as well. Your education is not over. It is still just beginning.

On the other hand, we fear that we have given you too much. And that brings me to my second point.

Resist legalism

The second piece of concluding advice that Paul offers is: Resist legalism. At the beginning of chapter 3, Paul gives a strongly worded warning about the temptations of legalism. With descriptively harsh words he denounces the Judiazers who wanted to offer circumcision as a crutch to be trusted in the journey of faith.

Now we don't get very excited about circumcision these days. Yet I suggest that we can easily be seduced by other forms of legalism. What do we mean by legalism today? I suggest that legalism includes anything upon which you depend in your walk with God other than Christ — or viewed from another perspective, anything which you allow to separate yourself from a brother or sister who is also seeking to follow Christ — anything which you believe makes you a better Christian than someone else.

If you accept these two components of my definition of legalism, you can see that those very things about which we are most spiritually passionate may well be the seeds of legalism, insinuating themselves between us and total dependence upon Christ — between us and our partners in the community of faith. Elements of our Christian life today that have the dangerous potential of becoming trusted structures and separating forces may include denominations (perhaps even transdenominationalism), models of worship (even in the Regent chapel), expressions of piety, social issues, even theological doctrine. Anything that might become a seductive substitute or even a temporary crutch for a relationship of uncontrollable trust in the grace of God offered in Christ is legalism.

Anything that allows me to define others who seek to follow Christ as less Christ-like than me is a dangerous form of legalism and a cancer in Christian community. One of the subtle dangers of any legalistic structure added to our faith is that it becomes a mark of distinction that separates us from others on the journey of faith — others seeking to work out their own relationship with God in Christ. This is an especially easy seduction for those of us in the evangelical side of the Church. We have strong beliefs, fervent commitments and articulated opinions. And these are good. But when they become more important that the relationship between a person and God in Christ, I think they take on the nature of legalism and become dangerous.

In my study of leadership I have been reflecting on the need to blend Christian community and effective organization in the administration of the church and its related institutions like Regent. Those who have taken my course know that one of my passions is a commitment that an effective "Christian" organization — to the extent that there is such a thing — must be *both* an effective mission-driven organization and a kingdom community reflecting the fruit of the spirit in its daily life. One of the difficulties in this marriage, however, is that organizations by definition are exclusive while kingdom community must by definition be inclusive.

Organizations require us to exclude those who do not enable us to achieve the mission that brings the organization into existence. Regent College, for example, has a carefully described profile of the kind of person who can be appointed to the faculty in the pursuit of our mission. We are exclusive. The danger comes when Regent or any other organization begins to think that our exclusive organizational parameters are coterminous with the kingdom community! The tragedy of Waco, Texas illustrates this in extreme. There are many whom we embrace inclusively as brothers and sisters in the kingdom who we would not appoint to the faculty and staff of the College. Our exclusive identity is important. But it must never separate us from those outside who are also seeking to follow Christ. This is a danger for us that needs to be underlined.

Last month Jim Packer, Don Lewis and I met with two senior Bishops of the Anglican Church about Regent's recognition by this denomination. While little was accomplished officially to move forward, I hope that we did make some headway relationally with them. One of their primary concerns was what I would call the legalism of Regent graduates. Noting the evangelical perspective of Regent, they stated that Regent graduates frequently treated them and their less evangelical colleagues as though they were not members of the same Church or following the same Lord. They added quite correctly that an Anglican priest, or layperson for that matter, placed in a parish in Castlegar or Kootanny does not have the luxury of choosing between St. John's Shaughnessy and St. Mary's. All Anglican's attend one parish church. Can a Regent alum serve and minister effectively to the whole spectrum of persons who comprise the Anglican communion? Or are they only able to serve evangelicals? We assured him that our graduates were inclusive in their kingdom service. I hope we were right!

The very education we have spent this past year encouraging you to pursue can become a barrier to your faith. If your new understanding of theology, your improved exegesis of biblical texts, your accumulation of historical data or your deepened awareness of your own spiritual growth becomes a substitute for emptying yourself in total humility before God in your relationship with Christ then it has failed you. If your education at Regent College separates you from the personal journey of other men and women in the marketplace or in the pews then it would be better that you had not enrolled.

Resist legalism. Hold everything in an open hand of humble submission before God, encouraging one another and those outside this community in their life with Christ in this world.

The third instruction with which I think Paul would send you out is …

Focus on your walk with Christ

Focus on Christ. For Paul this is the bottom line. This takes precedence over all else. It is Christ that he seeks to know. It is his walk with Christ that gives purpose to his life. It is Christ that causes him to discount all that he has accomplished. It is the righteousness of Christ that gives him hope and draws him on. It is his relationship with Christ that draws him into Good Friday and through Easter into the hope of resurrection life. It is this hope in the resurrection life, in the transformation of the body, that gives Paul peace as he sits under arrest and ponders the possibility of his own death.

Easter hope. This is the pull that draws us ahead on our journey. This is the hope that gives definition to our existence. It is both the inheritance that we anticipate and the power to live redemptively in this present world. We talk a lot about spirituality at Regent — about our walk with God, our desire to grow in the knowledge of Christ, to live in the power of his Spirit. It is this Easter hope that empowers us to seek to bring all of our life under the Lordship of Christ, to manifest the presence of Christ to those around us.

We live in a world without much hope. This was portrayed poignantly by the story last week of another child who committed suicide in a Native American community in Ontario. This was the 11th child to commit suicide in this little community since January! When other children were asked why this was happening, they responded, "Why not! What hope do we have!?" No hope . . .

A quick scan of the newspaper or review of the nightly news on television reinforces this pessimism. Last week's *Maclean's Magazine* featured a Bible on the cover with the bold title "God is Alive". Yet inside were articles on the murder of a pro-choice doctor, death in Somalia, a murderous election in Jamaica, the ravaging of Bosnia, angry strikes across the European Community, the shaky government of Russia and increasing unemployment in Canada. Peter Newman sarcastically brings the cover story together with the rest of the magazine when he writes, "Most Canadian executives' idea of spirituality these days is to pray every night that they'll have a job the next morning."

We know the cover story is correct. God is alive and at work in this world. But we also see a world seemingly set to self-destruct — a world in which life has lost its value.

This is the world you have been called to. This is the world you go out into as you leave this community. It is a world that desperately needs to meet and know the Christ who gives you hope. And yet it is a world that can suck that hope right from your soul if you take your eyes off of Christ. Paul understood this as he pondered the cross and his own possible death.

We have participated in your theological education. Hopefully we have contributed to the increase of your knowledge. But I pray that we have given you the space to grow in your walk with God — that we have encouraged your encounter with Christ — that we have nurtured the spiritual maturing of your soul. Your education will assist you in thinking theologically and biblically about that part of the world in which God places you. But it is your relationship with God in Christ that will keep you empowered by a hope that can be contagious. Don't stop in your journey and don't take your eyes off of Christ. Retain and nourish the habits and disciplines you developed while you were here. Spend time with God. As Paul wrote, "Press on to take hold of that for which Christ Jesus took hold of you . . . Stand firm in the Lord."

And finally,

Your character is your true diploma

The diploma that you receive at Convocation can be framed and nailed to your wall. Everyone who reads it will know that you have completed a rigorous course of study, that you are formally equipped to bring your faith to bear on the needs of the world. But most people will never read your Regent diploma and those who do will not take it as a measure of your spirituality. Rather it is your character that they will read. It is the presence of the spirit of Christ within you, shaping and moulding your character, that declares where you are in your walk with Christ.

Paul is not impressed with pedigree or achievement — only with the presence of Christ. He appeals to his friends in Philippi to "live up to what they have already attained." At different points in his letters Paul lists different fruit or manifestations of the spirit within the believer. As he brings this letter to a close, it is not hard to see again a profile of Christ-like character that for him reflects the depth of one's dependence upon God, the seriousness of one's walk with Christ, the reality of one's heavenly citizenship.

"Rejoice in the Lord always." The life characterized by a relationship with Christ will be a life of *rejoicing*. A life defined by a deep sense of joy and confidence in God that permeates all that we do — believing in God's ultimate

long range purpose and victory and communicating this joy by holding up visions of hope for those around us.

"Let your gentleness be evident to all." The life characterized by a relationship with Christ will be a life of *gentleness,* giving way graciously, not insisting on our own rights, using our education, our gifts and resources with love and humility and grace.

"The Lord is near." The life characterized by a relationship with Christ will be a life of *anticipation and expectation.* Paul is aware of the presence of Christ with him even under arrest. The Lord is near — he has not left you alone in this world. Paul also awaits his return and the transformation of this life.

It is the anticipation of what is yet to come and the expectation that God is with us now that should enable us to *"not be anxious about anything."* The life characterized by a relationship with Christ will be a life *free from anxiety* — a life of no worries. In a world of uncertainty this one is tough! Personally I have a long way to go to live up to what I believe here. It is one of many places where I need someone around who cares enough to remind me to stop worrying, to not be anxious. Both Beverly and Jean seem to work at this full-time. But if Christ is really with us, we need to learn to relax in his presence — to acknowledge our dependence and trust him — for the present as well as the long run.

"Pray with thanksgiving" The life characterized by a relationship with Christ will be a *thankful life* — a life that acknowledges continuously its total dependence upon God with expression of gratitude.

"And the peace of God will guard your hearts and your minds in Christ Jesus." The life characterized by a relationship with Christ will be a *peaceful life* — knowing that God is for us and in him we have our security — relaxing in God, caring for one another in a strife-free environment. God is not anxious. God knows what is going on and he's not anxious. It is this peace of God that is offered us and which in return should characterize our life.

Finally, the life characterized by a relationship with Christ will be a life *searching for excellence.* In 1982, a new paradigm in leadership expectations was launched with the publishing of the book *In Search of Excellence.* The authors called for leaders and managers who care for people and lead out of value-centered lives. They wanted to turn the focus of business from the bottom line of profit to the value line of people investment. Paul ends his letter with this same reminder to his readers and perhaps to himself. As he awaits his judgement, reviewing his life and ministry, struggling with the tensions and problems still plaguing the church, he reminds himself and us not to focus on the problems. Focus on the good things. Focus on what God is in fact doing in this world. Focus on things that are true, noble, right, pure, lovely, admirable and excellent. Fill your mind with the things of God and the God of peace will be with you. These are marks of the spiritual life. This is the diploma that counts. Your character reveals the depth of your theological education.

Final words of wisdom from the Apostle Paul to his fellow believers in Philippi. Final thoughts for a community about to break for the summer, for graduates about to take their hard earned theological education out into the world, in the marketplace and in the church to make a difference. Don't rest on your education; your journey is not done. Resist legalism — walk humbly before God and men and women. Focus on your walk with Christ as the ground of the hope you take into this world. And let your character be the true diploma for your time at Regent.

May the God who was at work in you to bring you to this community, and who has been shaping us all as we journeyed this year together, go with you and empower you with his presence that you might make a difference in the lives of the men and women that he is preparing to cross your path in the days ahead.

Regent Chapel
April 20, 1993

17

The Character of Christian Community

*S*ince, then, you have been raised with
Christ, set your hearts on things above,
where Christ is seated at the right hand of
God. Set your minds on things above, not
on earthly things. For you died, and your life is now hidden
with Christ in God. When Christ, who is your life appears,
then you also will appear with him in glory.

Put to death, therefore, whatever belongs to your
earthly nature: sexual immorality, impurity, lust, evil desires
and greed, which is idolatry. Because of these, the wrath
of God is coming. You used to walk in these ways, in the
life you once lived. But now you must rid yourselves of all
such things as these: anger, rage, malice, slander and filthy
language from your lips. Do not lie to each other, since you
have taken off your old self with its practises, and have put
on the new self, which is being renewed in knowledge in the
image of its Creator. Here there is no Greek or Jew, circumcised or uncircumcised, barbarian, Scythian, slave or free,
but Christ is all, and is in all.

Therefore, as God's chosen people, holy and dearly
loved, clothe yourselves with compassion, kindness, humility, gentleness and patience. Bear with each other and

forgive whatever grievances you may have against one another. Forgive as the Lord forgave you. And over all these virtues put on love, which binds them all together in perfect unity.

Let the peace of Christ rule in your hearts, since as members of one body you were called to peace. And be thankful. Let the word of Christ dwell in you richly as you teach and admonish one another with all wisdom, and as you sing psalms, hymns and spiritual songs with gratitude in your hearts to God. And whatever you do, whether in word or deed, do it all in the name of the Lord Jesus, giving thanks to God the Father though him.

Colossians 3:1-17

Good morning! It's a new year. We are a new community forming to study, to grow, to worship and to care for one another. As I said at Pre-Term, God is about to write another chapter in the story of Regent College as he uses this new community gathered in Vancouver to continue his shaping of each of us as leaders in his kingdom — men and women equipped to integrate our faith with our life and work — people empowered to make a difference in this world.

We are a community — at least we are in the process of becoming a community. And that's what I would like to talk about this morning. What does it mean to be a community? What is this "Regent College community" that we hear so much about? In the next few minutes I would like to explore with you four characteristics of Christian community, which I believe reflect the kind of community we want to be at Regent.

Regent College is an empowering community of Christian people committed to equipping you to live and work as a mature follower of Christ. All of us who live and work in this community can attest to the freeing, empowering and caring character of this community. But Regent is also a diverse collection of men and women struggling to learn to live and work together in Christian community. This is not heaven! We will not always live up to your expectations. But with your help we will continue to grow together in our maturity.

So, let's look at four characteristics of Christian community.

1. A community of focus
2. A community of diversity
3. A community of sinners
4. A community of accountability

A community of focus

My son has a submarine simulation game for his computer. In this game if you want to move the submarine to a new position in the ocean, you select a *waypoint* — a distant objective and lock the computer onto it. Regardless what comes across your path, the submarine continually moves toward its *waypoint*.

I have no idea whether that is the way it works in a real submarine. Fortunately my experience with submarine travel is limited to the game. But I do know that a similar concept is used in mountaineering navigation. Once mountaineers have determined their *bearing* — the direction that they want to head — they no longer rely only on the compass in their hand. They look up and focus on what could be called a *waypoint* in the distance and continue to walk towards that point. Compass readings will vary as you move around lakes, hills and ridges, but if you keep fixed on the waypoint you can continue making progress toward your goal.

Christian community is something like this. In today's world we come into community so needy that we frequently see it primarily as a support system — and it is. But if a group is formed simply to care for one another, it is not necessarily a Christian community.

Christian community is characterised by a common unity of focus, a common focus around which all its members unite. As Paul states so clearly that focus is Christ. Like a good submarine captain or mountaineering guide, Paul challenges us to "set our hearts and our minds on things above, where Christ is seated at the right hand of God."

If you are looking for Christian community at Regent College, you will find it first by focusing intentionally and intensely upon Christ and your relationship with him and in that act will find yourself standing side-by-side with others of us doing the same.

A community of diversity

We come together with a common focus, but we come as a diverse collection of believers. We represent different geographic regions of the world, different cultures, different vocations and professions, different church affiliations, different economic situations, men and women, younger and older persons, new believers and seasoned Christians. We come with different theological emphases, different modes of worship and prayer, different expressions of faith. This diversity exists on the Board, in the faculty and staff as well as in the student body. There is great diversity within the unity of our common focus — and that's the way it should be.

When Paul writes that "here there is no Greek or Jew, circumcised or uncircumcised, barbarian, Scythian, slave or free, . . ." he is not denying our diversity and arguing for a common uniformity. Rather he is acknowledging our differences and arguing against finding any special spiritual significance in your particular commitments. He is telling us that others who are different have something to offer and no particular approach to following Christ is of higher value. Christian community means giving people the space to become the persons God is forming. It resists putting definitions and models of Christian maturity upon one another. It resists trying to clone everyone else to be just like me.

Robert Fulghum, a minister and author in Seattle, captures this well in his story about the mermaid. Fulghum was leading a group of 80 children in a romping gymnasium game called Giants, Wizards, and Dwarfs. It's a large scale version of Rock, Paper and Scissors, and requires the kids to chose a group at a frenzied moment in the game. Fulghum writes:

> The excitement of the chase had reached a critical mass. I yelled out: "You have to decide now which you are — a Giant, a Wizard, or a Dwarf!" While the groups huddled in frenzied, whispered consultation, a tug came at my pants leg. A small child stands there looking up, and asks in a small concerned voice, "Where do the Mermaids stand?"
>
> Where do the Mermaids stand?
>
> A long pause. A very long pause. "Where do the Mermaids stand?" says I.

"Yes. You see, I am a Mermaid."

"There are no such things as Mermaids."

"Oh, yes, I am one!"

She did not relate to being a Giant, a Wizard, or a Dwarf. She knew her category. Mermaid. And was not about to leave the game and go over and stand against the wall where a loser would stand. She intended to participate, wherever Mermaids fit into the scheme of things. Without giving up dignity or identity. She took it for granted that there was a place for Mermaids and I would know just where. . . .

What was my answer at the moment? Every once in a while I say the right thing. "The Mermaid stands right here by the King of the Sea! says I. (Yes, right here by the King's Fool, I thought to myself.)

So we stood there hand in hand, reviewing the troops of Wizards and Giants and Dwarfs as they roiled by in wild disarray.

It is not true, by the way, that mermaids do not exist. I know at least one personally. I have held her hand.

(Robert Fulgham, *Everything You Need To Know,*
You Learned In Kindergarten. pp 83-85)

If we look for Christian community at Regent College, we will find it in the diversity of its members, each of whom has something to contribute to the texture of our fabric. If we can accept this diversity, we can learn from one another and enrich our own understanding of what it means to follow Christ.

A community of sinners

The third characteristic of community that is not always acknowledged. We are a community of sinners. Hard to believe when we sit here together for worship. Well scrubbed, well fed, well clothed, carrying our bibles and books, many coming to Regent from extensive ministry experience. We are the leaders of the Church. Yet Paul has to remind us to try to stop sinning and to live as

God's chosen people. He assumes we are sinners — forgiven . . . yes! — but still struggling with all of the desires, fears and hurtful forces within us. We are being renewed, but it is a continual swim up stream as we work hard (and usually secretly) to defeat our sinful side and put on the fruit of his spirit.

This summer Beverly and I were flying from Miami to Chicago. As the plane was being boarded in Miami, the seat across the aisle from me remained vacant. Just before flight time, a steward came in with a young man and showed him to that seat. Tall, lean, handsome, about 18 years old. His name was Georgi. At first he reminded me of my two sons. But the similarity quickly ended. Georgi had the mental and emotional capacity of a two-year old. His speaking was at the level of "Go see mommy. . . . Georgi go see mommy." For two hours I helped keep Georgi in his seat, kissed his three foot stuffed Mickey Mouse and continually refastened his seat belt. It was a long and emotional flight for me. On the outside, Georgi was a man. On the inside, Georgi was an infant too young to fly alone.

How like Georgi we are in the Church! On Sunday mornings we put on our good clothing, dust off our halo and process piously into worship. Yet inside we are struggling with life, with fears, doubts, failures, identity, purpose, direction. But we are afraid to let anyone know — because Christians are not supposed to be like that. So we play the Christian leader when inside we know we are still children trying to grow up in our faith.

These past years we have watched superstar Christian leaders toppled from their ministries because they were caught succumbing to their inner struggle. Over the past six months three persons of my acquaintance have stumbled in this struggle, damaging their reputation and ministry in variously sized circles.

To sit or stand here and pretend that we are different is a falsehood. I believe that every person in this room, faculty, staff and student, is engaged in this struggle. Each of us is working hard to work out our faith in this life — and the sad thing is that we often have to do it alone. We are afraid to show our failures, our weaknesses, our inability to live up to expectations for fear we will be rejected or not thought good enough to be a follower of Christ or a leader in the Church.

The irony is that the truth may be just the opposite. As Eugene Peterson points out, if you want to see a sinner, pick up the Bible and read about any of the great men and women of God. Struggling does not invalidate our ministry. In fact, it may be the necessary credential for credibility. We are a community of sinners and from the wisdom of Alcoholics Anonymous, we know that we need to confess that if we want to be healed.

A community of accountability

This brings us to the final characteristic I want to address today. A Christian community is also a community of accountability.

I like the story of Mark Wellman and Mike Corbett, two climbers who ascended El Capitan Peak in Yosemite Valley last year. After seven days of intense climbing on the massive rock face, they emerged at the summit to be greeted by the news media. The event was heralded by radio, TV and newspapers across North America.

What was so special about this climb? Hundreds of climbers ascend the face of El Capitan every year. The difference was in the climbers. Mark Wellman had attempted another climb in 1982 and had fallen. He was permanently paralysed from his waist down. He would never climb again. But Mark Wellman had a dream. He wanted to climb El Capitan. And Mark had a friend, a friend who believed in him, encouraged him, coached him and invested the time and energy necessary to get Mark to El Capitan.

The news media heralded the feat of Mark Wellman. I think we should spotlight also the role of Mike Corbett, the friend who tied himself to a paraplegic and encouraged him up one of the most daunting rock climbs in North America. The relationship between Mark Wellman and Mike Corbett represents for me one of the things that Christian community is all about. Mark Wellman could not hide his weakness and failure. He had to live with it. Mike Corbett did not shun his crippled friend. Rather, they roped up together, and together they overcame the limitations of Mark's weakness to grow together and accomplish their goal.

How much like mountaineering is living in community! We set our compass and fix our eyes upon the waypoint of Christ, rope ourselves to another who knows our weaknesses and loves us anyway, who accepts our limitations and encourages us to grow, as together we limp toward our objective — maturity in Christ.

Paul calls us to relationships of compassion, kindness, humility, gentleness and patience, bearing with each other and forgiving one another. Christian community, when it is working right, provides relationships on the human level that give us the space to grow and hold us accountable for that growth. Someone who knows us well and likes us anyway!

Two year's ago I joined this community as President. When I am introduced to outsiders as the President of Regent College there is usually a note of respect because Regent College is highly respected. I am treated as someone important — someone wise and spiritual, someone mature and confident who knows where he is going. And I am immediately struck by the dissonance within me. Because I do not think I am any of that.

When God placed me at Regent College he said "Look, I've given you some good experiences that will be helpful and I'm going to teach you a lot more . . . trust me." So I came. A simple person trying to follow his Lord — trying to learn what it means to be a president — like you, trying to grow before God in a community that God has blessed. I do it wrong occasionally — ask any member of the faculty, staff or board — but I'm learning and I know that I am totally dependent upon God if I am going to make any contribution to this College.

So, the first thing I did upon accepting this job was tighten my rope to God. I doubled the amount of time I spend each day in Scripture and prayer, and I fear to face any day without that important morning time.

Second, I lengthened some of the ropes I had with people. I have three such accountability relationships from my days in California. I know they pray for me continually and they regularly check in to see how I am doing. They know my strengths, my weaknesses, my fears and my hopes, and they like me anyway — and they let me know.

And third, I looked for new accountability relationships within the Regent Community with whom I could rope up. I am in the process of investing in several of these and growing together with the people involved. Let me note just three as examples.

My primary community of accountability at Regent is the Board of Governors. This is where I invest a significant amount of my time and where I would find my strongest rope link at present. Barry Hawes, the Chairman of the Board, made such a commitment to me from the beginning of my tenure, roping himself to me and I to him. We pray for each other daily, encourage each other regularly and are increasingly learning to trust one another with our struggles and our growth.

Similarly, Beverly and I joined a faculty support group nearly two years ago. This small group meets weekly for sharing, caring and prayer as we seek to encourage one another in our ministry and in our growth. With each meeting, trust grows and accountability increases.

And finally, I must mention Jean Sanson. Jean joined the Regent community at the same time that I did as my assistant. For two years we have been working together, trying to figure out what our jobs were and how to do them effectively. Because of our jobs we are roped up organizationally. But over two years, this has continued to build into one of my primary accountable relationships. Jean knows me as well as anyone in Canada and if you have met her you know she is quite capable of calling me to account!

Three relationships, plus old ones, in place to encourage my growth as they provide me with opportunities to invest in the growth of each of them.

Regent College wants to be the kind of community that creates and facilitates those kind of relationships. But it isn't easy. It's hard work. There is no instant community. Accountable relationships take time to build. Trust takes time — and it requires a lot of trust to rope your life to someone else, especially when you know that person has weaknesses just like you do and will probably fail you at times.

Such community is possible at Regent College. You can find such relationships in this community. But it will require two things from each one of us. First, a willingness to acknowledge that we are sinners, sinners undergoing renewal, but still sinners engaged in an ongoing struggle. Second, I believe that all accountability relationships start with one person investing in another. Personally empowering community is usually found when we reach out into another's life, learn to accept and love them for who they are in all their imperfections and commit ourselves to them. It is the return of such an investment that results in the kind of accountable relationships that give both persons the space and encouragement to grow.

You won't find this kind of life changing commitment in every relationship in which you invest, in every small group you join, in every worship service you attend. But if we as a college and as individuals commit ourselves to this level of relationship, every person in this community should find those whose lives will be enriched by your caring presence and, in the process of those investments, I believe that you will find persons who will walk with you in your struggle, encourage you in your journey of faith and hold you accountable for your growth in Christian maturity.

Focused on Christ, a diverse collection of sinners roped together can be a mighty community of witness in this city and around the world. May God bless this community this year and may he lead you into relationships in which you can encourage one another's growth in Christian maturity.

Regent Chapel
September 11, 1990

18

The Character of the Christian in Community

*P*aul, an apostle of Christ Jesus by the will of God, and Timothy our brother, To the holy and faithful brothers and sisters in Christ at Colosse: Grace and peace to you from God our Father.

We always thank God, the Father of our Lord Jesus Christ, when we pray for you, because we have heard of your faith in Christ Jesus and of the love you have for all the saints — the faith and love that spring from the hope that is stored up for you in heaven and that you have already heard about in the word of truth, the gospel that has come to you. All over the world this gospel is bearing fruit and growing, just as it has been doing among you since the day you heard it and understood God's grace in all its truth. You learned it from Epaphras, our dear fellow servant, who is a faithful minister of Christ on our behalf, and who also told us of your love in the Spirit.

For this reason, since the day we heard about you, we have not stopped praying for you and asking God to fill you with the knowledge of his will through all spiritual wisdom and understanding. And we pray this in order that you may live a life worthy of the Lord and may please him

in every way: bearing fruit in every good work, growing in
the knowledge of God, being strengthened with all power
according to his glorious might so that you may have great
endurance and patience, and joyfully giving thanks to the
Father, who has qualified you to share in the inheritance
of the saints in the kingdom of light. For he has rescued
us from the dominion of darkness and brought us into the
kingdom of the Son he loves, in whom we have redemp-
tion, the forgiveness of sins.

Colossians 1: 1-14

Last spring I was invited to give a lecture to the Executive Management Program of the University of Calgary. They wanted me to talk about organizational culture and leadership. The class was filled with senior executives from the oil patch in the Canadian prairies. The faculty was a little nervous. This was the first time they had invited a clearly identified representative from the religious community to speak to the class.

When I arrived they gave me biographies on each of the executives that would be participating in my seminar, pointing out to me that one in particular — Robert — might be a problem. He had indicated on his application that one of the resources he would bring to the university course was a focus on spirituality and values, coming out of his study of Judaism, Christianity and Zen. Up to this point in the course everyone had been avoiding Robert.

Apart from one or two questions and comments, Robert was relatively quiet during my seminar. The seminar went extremely well with most of the executives getting into a discussion of values in the marketplace and the leader's role in shaping values and culture within an organization. To the faculty's surprise, the class talked easily about issues of faith, values and beliefs and the relationship to their work. It was a very enjoyable discussion about leadership.

After lunch that day, however, Robert asked if he could talk with me and we had a very interesting conversation. It turns out that he had been raised a Christian but had become so disillusioned by the dissonance he saw between the values professed by Christians and the character he saw lived that he decided to look elsewhere. Robert's quest for a community that lived what he believed God expected led him to search through most of the world's religions. And he took his search seriously. He read avidly and attended a variety of worship and meditation experiences. At this stage in his life he had come back to the Christian faith, saw Jesus as the answer to his search, but still found it impossible to associate with the institutional church and most Christians because he did not see any integrity in their character. He sees Christians talking theology and piety and living out of a character that is less than Christian. Robert's relationship with God is very personal, slightly charismatic and results in intense dedication to his work as an engineer and to his colleagues.

Obviously his work has been noticed since every member of his department (most of his friends) were laid off in the energy industry cut backs except for him. He was sent to the seminar for promotion.

He is shunning the normal structures that we associate with an evangelical expression of faith, but he is striving hard to put his knowledge of God to work in his corner of the marketplace. Is he right?

While I think his reaction is extreme, I think his criticism hits home. The gap between what we profess and how we behave is often too great. We need to devote a little more energy to the development of Christian character if we want to enhance our witness in this world.

My conversation with Robert was not totally unrelated to the discussion we had had in the seminar. I had been talking about the culture of an organization. Every organization has its own culture — a set of beliefs and assumptions that control what actually happens in the life of the organization. Many organizations also have value statements or creeds that spell out what the organization commits to or professes as its values. In organizational life, a dissonance occurs when the stated values do not match the hidden culture, since the behaviours of an organization always reflect the culture. What's really important is acted out, not what we say is important.

One student here at Regent is doing a thesis on this topic, exploring how people get victimized in Christian organizations when they believe the stated values but find that the organization too often is operating on another unstated level. The most obvious example is the frequently stated value an organization attributes to its people when in reality most of them will sacrifice the people any day for the financial bottom line.

The culture of an organization shapes its behaviors. A good leader knows that it is impossible to plan or move intentionally into the future with an organization until one understands the culture out of which it operates. Because culture constrains strategy. You cannot plan beyond the walls of the culture, and the changing of culture is a long slow process.

Now, you might be wondering: what does organizational culture have to do with Christian character? The step from culture to character is only a move of particularization. What culture is to the organization, I am coming to believe, is what character is to the individual. If *culture* is the hidden system of assumptions and beliefs that control the behaviours of the organization, then *character* is the internalized set of assumptions, beliefs and commitments that control the behaviour of the individual. If the analogy holds, then we cannot move ahead in our Christian lives, we cannot grow in our maturity or our with one another until we come to grips with our character. In some ways it does not matter how accurate our statement of theological orthodoxy is or how visionary our plan of ministry if our character does not reflect those beliefs that we profess.

I think this is what Paul is getting at in his letter to the Colossians. He is addressing a Christian community whose faith is being challenged and whose Christian behaviour is about to be tested.

Paul is warning the Colossians about some in their midst who are claiming a "spiritual superiority," an access to spiritual knowledge through mysticism and rigorous attention to their own defined forms of piety, denying the full knowledge of God that is now available to everyone in the person and work of Jesus. The letter exalts Jesus as the Christ and brings everything to its focal point in Christ — that point where the believer is to fasten his or her hope, the hope, Paul says, that leads to a life of faith and love. The knowledge that we need for the development of our faith is found in our relationship with Christ. With this strong theological profession, Paul challenges the false teaching.

On the other side, Paul is about to test the Christian behaviour of his friends in Colosse by sending along with the letter, a runaway slave from one of their families who comes back now as a Christian brother. With Tychicus and the letter comes Onesimus with Paul's full endorsement

So what does Paul expect? What kind of life is he calling the Colossians to? I find the passage we read this morning helpful when I look at this question. Immediately following his prayer of thanksgiving for the strong faith and love that their hope has led them to demonstrate up to this point, he goes on to pray for them *"asking God to fill (them) . . . with the knowledge of his will through all spiritual wisdom and understanding, . . . in order that (they) . .*

. may live a life worthy of the Lord and may please him in every way." (1:9-10)
He prays for a knowledge of God that will be so internalized that it will shape
their very character and result in lives that are worthy of their Lord and pleas-
ing to him.

Paul then goes on to explain what he is thinking about when he speaks of
living worthy of God. Verses 10-12 follow with four parallel participles that
define what is meant by living worthily or living with Christian character:
"bearing fruit in every good work," "growing in the knowledge of God," and I like
this next one, *"being strengthened with all power according to his glorious might."*
That's where we would like to stop the sentence . . . but Paul goes on to add
"so that you may have great endurance and patience." And finally, *"joyfully giving
thanks to the Father."*

In these four requests, I believe Paul outlines the expectations of Christian
character and, I trust, gives us an outline for what we are about at Regent
College. I would like to think students (and faculty) come to Regent College:
to learn to know God, to learn to bear fruit, to make a difference, to learn the
power of patience and to learn the perspective of gratitude. Let me comment
briefly on each of these platforms in Paul's prayer:

To learn to know God

This is the one we like to start with at Regent College because it reflects
the primary mandate of an educational institution. Knowledge is what we
are all about. I find it interesting that Paul, like Peter (2 Pet. 1:5), actually
puts it lower on the list. Peter's list starts with faith, then goodness and then
knowledge in what seems to be an escalating building of virtues. For Paul it is
almost as though the knowledge of God that confirms our faith comes out of
our action, out of our acts of goodness, our good works, the fruit or expression
of the spirit within us.

When Paul speaks about increasing our knowledge of God, he is talking
about more than intellectual inquiry. He is talking about a relationship with
God in Christ that lasts a lifetime, a long range commitment to continue in
faith, to hold onto the redeeming, reconciling hope represented by the Gospel
presented to us in Scripture and made alive by the presence of Christ in our
midst (1:23-27). Picking up language used by Eugene Peterson in *Run with the
Horses,* the knowledge of God is like a marriage not a wedding. (*Run with the*

Horses, p. 68) The false teachers proposed an easy access to knowledge, which Peterson would liken to the easy 30 minutes it takes to perform a wedding. Paul recognizes that we learn to know God like we engage a spouse in marriage. It is a lifetime relationship of hard work, of study, of prayer, of ministry, of success and failures. Again to use Peterson's words, it is "a long obedience in the same direction." The first foundation of Christian character is a lifetime commitment to know God, to seek the mind of Christ through his word and his spirit.

To learn to bear fruit

While we might want to start with knowledge, Paul puts at the top of his list of participles, *"bearing fruit in every good work."* He expects that faith will result in a character that produces active goodness that makes a difference in the world. In the third chapter of his letter, Paul spells out what the fruit of Christian character looks like when it enters the marketplace. The believer is one characterized by:

Compassion — that showing of mercy to another that reflects the grace and mercy that God has shown us; reaching out to another in undeserved care and commitment even as they fail to live up to our expectations.

Kindness — specific acts of goodness, coming out of all that God as given us, directed toward those around us; using the gifts that God has given us to the benefit of those with whom we have been placed in relationship.

Humility — that appropriate valuing of oneself in proper perspective before God, recognizing our creatureliness and our servanthood.

Gentleness — a willingness to absorb unto oneself the pain directed toward another. This is a quality exemplified by Jesus and, interestingly, a term used to describe Moses, who while leading in strength, was called upon to absorb the murmuring and hostilities of his colleagues.

Patience — that willingness to accept people where they are and work over the long haul toward their maturity — the ability to see them as God sees them, complete and mature in Christ.

Bearing with and forgiving one another — here Paul expects us to respond to people in process exactly the way we have been responded to by God — tolerance and forgiveness as God has forgiven us.

And unity — that common mind with one another based on our shared experience of the Gospel, our commitment to love and our participation in the peace of Christ.

This is the measure of our Christian maturity. These are the marks of our Christian character. And this is the winsome character that draws people to our message about what God has done in Christ.

The engineer I mentioned earlier — the one looking for people who reflected these marks of Christian character — referred me on to Graham Tucker. Graham Tucker is another engineer who was introduced to Christ by two of his fellow engineers whose faith he says was expressed not "in theological language, . . . (but) manifested in . . . relationships, values, attitudes, leadership style, and concern for people" (Graham Tucker, *The Faith-Work Connection*, p. 9). His pilgrimage led to ordination as an Anglican priest and then back into the marketplace where he first met God. He was the founding director of the King-Bay Chaplaincy in downtown Toronto, a lay oriented ministry to business men and women. He also established Operation Bootstrap, a program focusing on personal renewal, career counselling and job creation for people out of work, and at the time when I met with him he was currently setting up a Center for Business Ethics. Two Christian engineers whose personal character reflected the fruit of the Spirit have borne fruit for the kingdom that continues to unfold in the city of Toronto.

The second foundation of Christian character is a commitment to develop and express the marks of the spirit of Christ in every relationship in which God places us.

To learn the power of patience

This is the hard one. I am a contented product of an instant society. I want it now. Instant gratification is no longer a value for most of us. It is an expectation. When I decide to buy something, I want it to be in stock now. I do not want to order it! When I make a telephone call, I want to get through now. I can't stand busy signals or answering machines. Time has become a more important commodity than money. Before Beverly left for Taiwan several weeks ago, she showed me how to cook some of the necessary staples I would need to survive until she gets back. About half-way through her description on how to steam rice, I asked why we didn't use instant rice? Just leave me some instant rice, some instant oatmeal, some microwave dishes and a freezer full of chocolate chip cookies. I want to eat...not cook!

Now that is probably an overstatement, but it reflects a strong force within me. Instinctively, I do not have much patience. On the other hand, I began to learn about patience when I got involved in organizational leadership. Organizations are patient. When it comes to change, they can out wait anybody. Corporations are very difficult to change. Educational institutions are harder. The church is the hardest of all. The church can out wait Methuselah in its resistance to change!

If you want to effect lasting change in an organization, you need to take a longitudinal approach. Research has shown that organizational cultures — that controlling set of assumptions and beliefs that we mentioned earlier — can only be changed by systematic articulation and repeated reinforcement of a new vision or set of values. You cannot leap into a new future. You have to walk slowly and comfortably with people until they find themselves in the new future of their own accord. Then you have change that lasts. But it takes time. It requires patience. And yet that patience has the power to move the most rigid organization into a new life.

The same kind of patience is required in our relationships in community. Paul is probably thinking about the false teachers in the Colossian community. He knows the Colossians will need patience and endurance to stand up to the attacks and opposition they will face. But he might also be thinking about the patience and long range endurance that will be required to love those false teachers back into the community. He might even be thinking about the patience Onesimus will need as he waits for Philemon and the Colossians to transform their thinking about him from that of slave to that of Christian brother. People relationships require patience. Patience is that ability to accept people where they are and walk with them on their path of renewal and growth — believing in their future and holding them accountable to their development. Such patience often does require us to be strengthened with the full power of God's might, but such patience has the power to see a person grow in grace and in a fullness of maturity in Christ.

The third foundation of Christian character is a commitment to refocus ourselves from short-term myopia to God's eternal perspective and unleash the power of patience in the community of relationships around us.

The perspective of gratitude

When I enrolled at Fuller Seminary as a new seminarian, I was assigned a prayer mother. Betty Junvik and her husband Bengt committed themselves to encourage and pray for me daily during my seminary studies. I am sure she didn't realize when she accepted this assignment that I would be a student at Fuller for 11 years! But she stood faithfully with me for the whole time.

About half-way through this time, Bengt, who was president of a company near Los Angeles, took vacation time to fly a small airplane from Seattle to a mission station in Alaska to deliver it to Mission Aviation Fellowship. In the course of his flight he disappeared. Search and rescue teams fanned out all over the Brooks Range which he had to cross to reach his destination. People all over the United States were praying for him. His son Bruce hired a team of helicopter pilots to conduct their own search. Nothing. No trace of him or the plane. As the days dragged on, it became clear to most that he would not be found. By the 13th day, the search and rescue operation was called off and he was given up for lost by everyone — except his son Bruce. Bruce would not accept his father's death and persuaded the helicopter team to make one last sweep the next day up several of the canyons that had already been searched. On their last leg they flew up a box canyon with no exit for a light plane. Upside down in the snow, its white belly blending in with the frozen landscape, was the plane and inside it was Bengt Junvik writing a last letter to his young daughter.

Many lives were changed that day — the Junvik family, the helicopter pilots and others from the search operations. But no one was changed as profoundly as Bengt Junvik. For Bengt, God had given him a new life, a second chance. When he recovered his strength, he sold his business and went around the United States telling people about life, about what God had done for him and had done for them. His story of thankfulness was an encouragement to thousands of people. Bengt Junvik now saw life from a different perspective. He looked at this world from the perspective of gratitude.

You cannot read the letter to the Colossians without being overwhelmed by Paul's sense of gratitude. From beginning to end, the letter communicates a perspective of gratitude. Paul is thankful about everything. He is giving praise and thanksgiving at every point. And with good reason. Not only is he thankful for the faith and love demonstrated by the Colossian church, for the conversion and service of Onesimus, for the ability to send these letters and have companions even while living in prison. More than that, he is overwhelmed with gratitude for all that God has done for him and for the world in Christ — for rescuing us, forgiving us, redeeming us, bringing us into the kingdom of his son and qualifying us to receive an inheritance as saints. And that is still

Chapter 1! It is that perspective of gratitude that permeates all that Paul does and writes. It is an absolute dependence upon God and revelling in what he has done and what he is doing today. Being thankful is an acknowledgement of dependence and the ground of hope.

Each summer I invite the summer school faculty to my home for dinner. I always ask them two questions: What is God doing in your world today? and What do you see in the next century that we should be preparing for in the years ahead? It is an encouragement to all of us to be reminded of how much God is still doing today and how much we are dependent upon him as we move into the future. The perspective of gratitude is a perspective of humility, of dependence, of confidence in God and hope for the future.

The fourth foundation of Christian character is the commitment to relax and rejoice in the grasp of God in Christ with thanksgiving. It is the perspective from which we move confidently into the future, praying that God will fill us with the knowledge of his will through all spiritual wisdom and understanding that we might live a life worthy of the Lord and may please him in every way — learning to know God all of our life — learning to bear fruit that makes a difference — learning the power of patience in every relationship — learning the perspective of gratitude that leads to dependence and hope. May God sustain in you a Christian character that reflects his presence in your life, your work and your relationships.

Regent Retreat
September 30, 1990

19

Accountability in Community

*H*ow would you feel? You are a respectable lay leader in your church — a person known for the care and commitment you shower on others in your congregation — a person who actively participates in and supports the development of community in your church fellowship. People are refreshed in their faith because of your leadership and the depth of your relationship with Christ.

But you've had some problems lately. A member of your personal staff has betrayed you. A person you trusted has stolen from you and left town. What hurts worse — the loss of a good worker? The theft of your property? The betrayal by someone to whom you gave your trust?

This event has not affected your leadership in the church, but it has hurt you personally. Perhaps you still carry a little anger, perhaps a lot of anger! You were betrayed. Now you understand a little what Jesus felt when Judas turned against him.

Then one morning you look up and see two men coming toward you. One is the thief. How do you feel? What emotions run through your mind? Revenge? Repayment? Justice? Your fist clenches. Your stomach tightens. Your heart speeds up. Now finally you can take care of this matter that has been eating at you — this hurt and anger that you have been carrying around.

But who is this other guy? Isn't that someone we've seen with Paul?

Tychicus, I think his name was. What's he doing here? Perhaps he found out about that scoundrel and has drug him back here to see justice.

And yet something seems wrong here as Tychicus greets you on behalf of himself and Paul. Your runaway staff person is watching you with a strange look in his eyes — a mixture of love and sadness. But not fear. Why not? You can have his head for what he did to you.

And then Tychicus hands you the letter . . . a personal letter from Paul who is in prison. You read the letter:

> *Paul, a prisoner of Christ Jesus, and Timothy our brother,*
>
> *To Philemon our dear friend and fellow worker, to Apphia our sister, to Archippus our fellow soldier and to the church that meets in your home,*
>
> *Grace to you and peace from God our Father and the Lord Jesus Christ.*
>
> *I always thank my God as I remember you in my prayers, because I hear about your faith in the Lord Jesus and your love for all the saints. I pray that you may be active in sharing your faith, so that you will have a full understanding of every good thing we have in Christ. Your love has given me great joy and encouragement, because you, brother, have refreshed the hearts of the saints.*
>
> *Therefore, although in Christ I could be bold and order you to do what you ought to do, yet I appeal to you on the basis of love. I then, as Paul — an old man and now also a prisoner of Christ Jesus — I appeal to you for my son Onesimus, who became my son while I was in chains. Formerly he was useless to you, but now he has become useful both to you and to me.*
>
> *I am sending him — who is my very heart — back to you. I would have liked to keep him with me so that he could take your place in helping me while I am in chains for the gospel. But I did not want to do anything without your consent, so that any favour you do will be spontaneous and not forced. Perhaps the reason he was separated from you for a little while was that you might have him back for*

good — no longer as a slave, but better than a slave, as a dear fellow believer in the Lord.

So if you consider me a partner, welcome him as you would welcome me. If he has done you any wrong or owes you anything, charge it to me. I, Paul, am writing this with my own hand. I will pay it back — not to mention that you owe me your very self. I do wish, brother, that I may have some benefit from you in the Lord; refresh my heart in Christ. Confident of your obedience, I write to you, knowing that you will do even more that I ask.

And one thing more: Prepare a guest room for me, because I hope to be restored to you in answer to your prayers.

Epaphras, my fellow prisoner in Christ Jesus, sends you greetings. And so do Mark, Aristarchus, Demas and Luke, my fellow workers.

The grace of the Lord Jesus Christ be with your spirit.

Paul

Subtly, lovingly, but clearly, Paul is sending you a message. Things have changed with Onesimus, your runaway slave. He is now a Christian brother. Everything that you have been teaching and preaching at church, sharing with your friends at work is suddenly being put to the test. Participation in the fellowship of *koinonia* is no longer a theoretical theological concept of our common fellowship in Christ. It is now a demanding expectation of your faith. What you have been teaching as a commitment of your faith, you are now being asked to demonstrate in relationship to a person who has betrayed your trust.

It's as though Paul is saying: "OK, Philemon, let's see if you really believe what you have been talking about. Your faith should make a difference in your life. Now is the time to see if that works. Reinstate Onesimus — not just back on your staff — but also as a Christian brother. This is your chance to model what you believe!"

With a masterful stroke of his pen, Paul has confronted Philemon with the implications of his faith. The Christian love for which he is so well known, all comes down now to how he will deal with Onesimus. Paul expects the Gospel to make a difference. He expects with confidence that Philemon will be able to transcend his sense of offence, his personal loss and his pain of betrayal and embrace Onesimus as a changed person and a Christian companion, reinstating him to his staff and taking the risk to give him his trust again.

Now what does this have to do with us sitting here this morning, beginning a new academic year in the pursuit of theological education? Three things, I think:

1. Theological education includes character building.
2. Community is the context for character building.
3. Community requires individual effort and risk.

Theological education includes the building of character as well as intellect

For the next months you will be deeply engaged in the rigors of your academic programs. You will be learning language, exegeting scripture, reviewing history, developing your theology, sharpening your skills and gaining a Christian perspective on the world around us. When you have completed your program at Regent, we hope we will have given you a basic foundation for your faith, an intellectual approach to the integration of your faith and your life. We hope you will have learned to think and to understand what it means to be a Christian at the turn of the century.

But if this is all you learn at Regent College, we will have failed.

Philemon knew his faith. He had a reputation for goodness and piety. But Paul wanted more. He wanted Philemon's faith to have permeated his total being in such a way that it changed the way he lived — faith that makes a difference. Faith that can see Jesus in the eyes of the person who has betrayed your trust and hurt you personally. Faith that responds out of a Christ shaped character.

It is not enough that you leave Regent with a graduate diploma and a solid intellectual grasp of your faith. It is only enough if your faith makes a difference in the way you live. We are interested in developing your orthodoxy as theologians. We are committed to your growth in the practice of piety. But, like Paul, we expect more. We want to contribute to your spiritual growth in Christ so that you *live what you believe.* Theology that stays in the head or is expressed only in a religious context is not enough. Biblical theology, according to Paul, results in changed lives in everyday living. Everything that

Philemon taught about his faith was now on the line in the way he responded to Onesimus, a member of his staff. Had his faith truly shaped his character in a way that God could reach through him to Onesimus? This was a teaching moment in the life of the Colossian community.

Similarly, everything you study at Regent College will be put to the test every day in the way you live, the way you do business, the way you parent, the way you walk with friends or relate to strangers. The teaching moment at Regent College is more likely to come at a point of personal tension than in the exchange of a classroom. As God works in and through us, we begin to understand what this theological education is all about. It is learning to see Jesus in the lives of those around us. It is letting the person and love of God touch others through you. It is meeting God in the context of an empowering community united in Christ.

Community is the context for character building

This brings me to the second point I find in this story: Community is the context for character building. It is in the context of the Colossian community that the relationship between Philemon and Onesimus will be worked out. In this carefully worded letter to Philemon, Paul tells us at least three things about this community that provides the context for building character — three things that we should note as we commit ourselves to live and work together for this next year or two.

First, *Christian community includes all kinds of people.* For Philemon this was a dramatic revelation. A person who was once his slave, he must now see as a fellow believer in the community. What will this mean? How does an upper middle class church leader relate to an uneducated runaway slave?

Our diversity is not as dramatic, but it is varied. The community that is forming at Regent this year represents over 30 different countries and cultures, 75 different church or denominational backgrounds, a variety of vocations, a mixture of age and experience, different levels of social-economic opportunity.

Part of the richness of our year together is the contribution that this diversity can bring to the education of each person in the community. Yet it also requires additional effort as people from different points work to understand each other and you work to build from your common faith to genuine friendship that transcends yet encompasses the diversity.

I encourage you to take the risk of reaching into someone else's world. Avoid the temptation to hang around only with your own. The investment of seeking to learn from the differences of those around you can only enrich your understanding of the God you came here to engage in study.

The second thing we learn about community is that *Christian community can handle conflict.* It is in community that conflict is reconciled. Paul has certain expectations for Philemon and the Colossian Church in relationship to the conflict that Philemon has with Onesimus. His letter outlines a very powerful approach. I want to address the topic of conflict in the community more specifically in the next chapter.

Third, *Christian community takes precedence over personal agendas.* We started this morning looking at Philemon's feelings. He has a debt to settle with Onesimus, a personal agenda to take care of. Yet Paul is calling him back to his commitment to community. Paul reminds him of his reputation for supporting the community and encouraging its members — his faith, his love and his generous investment in the community at Colosse. Now Paul sends Onesimus back as a member of that community and expects Philemon's commitment to the community to take precedence over his own hurt, his own need for personal satisfaction.

Regent College is a community of over 500 personal agendas. I was reminded of a comment I heard a Regent professor make in response to a question last year. He made that statement that what made Regent different from other schools at which he had taught was the willingness of faculty to submit their strong personal agendas to the community agenda of the college.

Each of you has come to Regent for your own personal reasons this fall. I suggest that God's engagement in meeting your particular needs is directly related to your willingness to invest yourself in the lives of those around you in this community and your willingness to place your own agenda on a back burner or shelf. I believe that if we seek to reach out in the love of God to those around us, we will find that Jesus may well meet us in those very persons.

Community requires individual effort and risk

The third point I see in this story: Community requires individual effort and risk. Community doesn't just happen. People make it happen. Paul made it happen by standing between two separated members. Onesimus made it happen by taking the risk to return and invest himself. Philemon will make it happen by putting his personal agenda behind him.

Christian community is an interesting paradox. It finds its foundation in one person, Jesus Christ, in whom individuals participate in the koinonia of the spirit, one-on-one in relationship to God in Christ. And yet it is this shared individual experience, this common participation in the Spirit of Christ that brings us into community, the koinonia of the spirit. And it is in this community that we are called to reach out to others in one-on-one relationships that allow God to work through us mediating Christ to one another.

While the starting point and the end product of a specific Christian community is a corporate expression of the body of Christ in this particular place, living in community requires each person to take the risk to invest him or herself in other persons. It requires an intentional effort and entails risk. Any effort to reach out to another risks rejection, hurt and possibly betrayal. It also offers the possibility of love, acceptance, accountability and encouragement.

The initiative to make community happen here at Regent College is in each of your hands. Onesimus had to risk to reach out to Philemon. The initiative was in his hand. Now Philemon must respond. Whether or not Regent becomes a community context for the shaping of your character in the process of theological education remains initially in your hands. You have one living person to invest in this community. Take the risk. Invest yourself in the people sitting around you this morning and see what God does with your investment.

The formal process of theological education is very self-centered. You will be graded and affirmed on what you alone have learned and how well you can express that learning. But it is the community of fellow believers who provide you with the context in which to invest and test your learning. If you learn anything at Regent College this year, I pray that it will be to let God work through you and for you in the community of men and women that he has gathered here this year as one expression of the body of his Son, our Lord.

May you meet God in Christ in the most unlikely of relationships as this year unfolds.

Regent Chapel
September 10, 1991

20

Conflict in Community

*L*et's go back to the story of Philemon and Onesimus and the Colossian Church. Imagine yourself in a meeting of the Colossian Church shortly after Tychicus and Onesimus arrived with Paul's letters to Philemon and to the Colossians — a gathering much like this one. The church has assembled in the home of one of the elders. People are sitting around, some on chairs, some on the floor, some standing. A new letter has been received from Paul written from prison.

In a day without Bibles this was a major event. The letter will be read today and a word from God will be received through the apostle Paul. There is an air of excitement and anticipation throughout the congregation.

But there is also an ripple of anxiety and discomfort. You can feel the tension. Sitting in the room are Philemon and Onesimus. Philemon, one of the leaders of this church, was betrayed last year by one of his family slaves who stole from him and ran away. Philemon had been very upset about the experience and had shared it with the congregation.

And now, here sits Onesimus, the runaway slave — sent back as a believer — by Paul himself. We know that Philemon also received a personal letter from Paul. That must account for his willingness to have Onesimus here in the same room with him. Perhaps he will share Paul's letter with us.

How are we supposed to deal with this? Onesimus is a slave! Should he be here? And yet he seems to be a genuinely converted believer — and he has Paul's blessing. Should we let Christian slaves into our church? And what about his crime? He stole from Philemon and ran away. That's punishable by death. Do we ignore that? Apparently Paul wants Philemon to take Onesimus back into his house, reinstate him as a member of his staff and accept him as a Christian brother.

What's our role in this? We are their community. We are supposed to be the body of Christ. We know that Philemon is an important and active member of this community. And now we need to embrace Onesimus. How do we do this? How do we deal with the conflict that is obviously going on in a lot of minds in this room?

Can this really be of God if it is causing all this conflict for us?

It's not hard to imagine that kind of scene on the Sunday after Tychicus and Onesimus arrived. Sitting in their place, let's listen to parts of the letter to the Colossians, keeping in mind that Philemon and Onesimus are sitting here listening as well.

> *Since, then, you have been raised with Christ, set your hearts on things above, where Christ is seated at the right hand of God. Set your minds on things above, not on earthly things. For you died, and your life is now hidden with Christ in God. When Christ, who is your life appears, then you also will appear with him in glory.*
>
> *Put to death, therefore, whatever belongs to your earthly nature: sexual immorality, impurity, lust, evil desires and greed, which is idolatry. Because of these, the wrath of God is coming. You used to walk in these ways, in the life you once lived. But now you must rid yourselves of all such things as these: anger, rage, malice, slander and filthy language from your lips. Do not lie to each other, since you have taken off your old self with its practises, and have put on the new self, which is being renewed in knowledge in the image of its Creator. Here there is no Greek or Jew, circumcised or uncircumcised, barbarian, Scythian, slave or free, but Christ is all, and is in all.*
>
> *Therefore, as God's chosen people, holy and dearly loved, clothe yourselves with compassion, kindness, humility, gentleness and patience. Bear with each other and forgive whatever grievances you may have against one*

another. Forgive as the Lord forgave you. And over all these virtues put on love, which binds them all together in perfect unity.

Let the peace of Christ rule in your hearts, since as members of one body you were called to peace. And be thankful. Let the word of Christ dwell in you richly as you teach and admonish one another with all wisdom, and as you sing psalms, hymns and spiritual songs with gratitude in your hearts to God. And whatever you do, whether in word or deed, do it all in the name of the Lord Jesus, giving thanks to God the Father though him.

Wives, submit to your husbands, as is fitting in the Lord.

Husbands, love your wives and do not be harsh with them.

Children, obey your parents in everything, for this pleases the Lord.

Fathers, do not embitter your children, or they will become discouraged.

Slaves, obey your earthly masters in everything; and do it, not only when their eye is on you and to win their favour, but with sincerity of heart and reverence for the Lord. Whatever you do, work at it with all your heart, as working for the Lord, not for human masters, since you know that you will receive an inheritance from the Lord as a reward. It is the Lord Christ you are serving. Those who do wrong will be repaid for their wrongs, and there is no favouritism.

Master, provide your slaves with what is right and fair, because you know that you also have a Master in heaven.

Colossians 3:1-4:1

Powerful words for a church struggling with conflict. But what does this have to do with us nearly two thousand years later? Do we ever have conflict in our Christian community?

As many of you know, I regularly participate in white water canoe trips or mountain climbing. My partner, Don, and I have been roped together or shared a canoe now for nearly 17 years. We have grown close in this time, learned to trust each other and to care deeply about each other's lives.

Do we ever experience conflict? Only every time the canoe heads over a rapids with me in the front! Don and I are both opinionated, controlling persons with very definite ideas how to get through the water and rocks alive. However, I sit in the front. I am the first to taste the rapids, and when my paddle goes into the water, I have a major effect on the control of the canoe whether Don agrees or not. Don and I have debated procedures before, during and after successful runs and total disasters. We have experienced many conflicts. But we care for each other and have linked our survival by roping up on the mountain or sharing the canoe on the river. We both have a vested interest in the best outcome and are willing to confront each other on our behaviours and procedures and listen to the other person carefully. Failure to listen usually ends up with one or both of us swimming down stream!

Close community includes conflict. But caring relationships work for the resolution of conflict and the growth of community. I would like to comment this morning on conflict, confrontation, criticism and gossip in the Christian community, and see if we can learn something from the way Paul approached this situation.

First of all, *should there be conflict in a Christian community?* Let's look at conflict. What is it? Conflict, as the psychologists tell us, is not something that happens between two people. It is something that happens in us as individuals when we encounter differences, something that does not fit our understanding of a situation.

Is conflict appropriate in Christian community? I suggest that it is probably a required corollary of community. The very definition of Christian community includes an acceptance of diversity — witness Philemon and Onesimus — and diversity means differences — differences of approach and values, of perspective and opinions, of expectations and hopes, of commitments. And difference causes conflict.

Conflict is not only possible in Christian community, it may be a necessary by-product of community that is an important catalyst for growth as we learn to adjust to the differences caused by the diversity of community. No conflict may suggest no diversity and possibly no growth. Both Philemon and Onesimus experienced conflict before and during their reconciliation and their presence probably produced conflict in many of the members of the

Colossian church. On this side of heaven, I believe there will always be conflict in Christian community as we struggle to learn to live like the body of Christ in this world.

But if conflict is inevitable, how do we handle it? Here I think Paul gives us a good model. A model I would call caring confrontation over against criticism and gossip. In the passage we read, he discards anger, rage, malice, slander as inappropriate characteristics for a Christian community — and affirms compassion, kindness, humility, gentleness, patience, forgiveness and love. It is clear that Paul sees a caring attitude of love dominating all community relationships. Yet he goes on to encourage the Colossians to engage one another in teaching and instruction or confrontation that emerges from their study of the God's word. I believe Paul expects confrontation, but he expects it to be conducted in the context of a caring relationship, a relationship in which both parties are genuinely concerned about the growth and development of each other in the community.

Let me distinguish between caring confrontation and criticism. I believe that *confrontation* addresses a person's behaviours or attitudes in light of *that person's stated values* or commitments — not *my* values or beliefs. Confrontation holds people accountable to live what they teach or claim as important. It does not address their progress by standards that I hold up for myself. If confrontation is to be effective or constructive, there must be a caring relationship surrounding it. Within the context of a caring relationship, you can hold me accountable to my own values and beliefs because I know that you care and want to see me grow in my faith.

On the other hand, *criticism*, I believe, attacks the other person without the supportive context of a caring relationship. Criticism may address a person's failure to live up to his or her commitments or beliefs, but with little genuine interest in the person's growth and development. Criticism, however, frequently focuses on my internal conflict. Because I am in conflict, I want you to change, not because I care about you, but because I am focusing on myself. Criticism may be directed to the person who is causing my conflict, but often is directed to someone else about that person.

Caring confrontation is concerned about the other person's growth and emerges within a relationship of trust. Criticism emerges from our own conflict and usually destroys trust. Confrontation wants to see positive growth. Criticism wants to express hurt and conflict. Confrontation usually seeks resolution. Criticism usually seeks removal of my conflict.

Now, you might ask: What about conflict caused because someone I care about has different values and beliefs — perhaps a non-believer? Confronting such a person might hold their behaviour accountable to their commitments but still miss what I consider to be appropriate Christian values.

That's a fair question, and everyone might not agree with my position. I believe that a person can only be held accountable to live up to the life that they have committed themselves to. I can care for them, I can share what I believe with them in the context of that caring, but I cannot judge them by my standards. I believe I am called to love them where they are. If in the development of our relationship I can convince you to adopt a new set of standards, beliefs or values, then I can loving hold you accountable to live up to your new stated commitments. That doesn't mean I lower my standards. And it is possible that I might have to sacrifice a relationship for what I believe. But I do very little for your growth or our relationship if I keep confronting you with your failure to live up to my expectations, to live by my Christian standards.

I think this is the genius of Paul's confrontation with Philemon. Read the letter again (Chapter 19) and watch how Paul underlines his deep love for Philemon — the caring relationship — and holds Philemon accountable to act according to Philemon's commitments.

In the context of a deep and caring relationship, Paul has confronted Philemon with the implications of his commitments. Philemon is known for his encouragement of fellow believers, for his participation in and support of community. And this is what Paul appeals to. He does not attack the institution of slavery. He does not hold Philemon accountable for a value system that we in this century think he should have understood. Rather, he stays within the values and culture of Philemon and the Colossian church, but he lovingly points out to Philemon that his commitment to community might require him to take a second look at his relationship with Onesimus.

I think we can learn something about caring confrontation in the way Paul writes to Philemon.

First, he clearly establishes the context of a caring relationship. There can be no question that Paul and Philemon are integrally bound up with one another in mutual respect and love.

Second, he brings Onesimus directly into that relationship by underlining his own deeply personal and spiritual relationship with the converted slave. Philemon can no longer deal with Onesimus as a personal offense or inhuman slave. Now he must deal with his relationship with Paul. It is Paul that he must see when he looks at Onesimus.

Third, Paul confronts Philemon with his own commitments. The opening prayer lifts up Philemon's contributions as a member of the Colossian community, his investment in the members of the church. The refreshment and encouragement for which Philemon is known, Paul now asks for himself, and through him for Onesimus.

Note that while there is strong expectation running throughout Paul's letter, there is no indication that the relationship with Philemon would be ended if Philemon does not comply. Paul resists using his authority, at least directly, and leaves it up to Philemon to decide how far he will go in his acceptance of Onesimus.

Fourth, Paul takes unto himself the cost of the confrontation. He assumes Onesimus' debt and offers to cover all costs due to Philemon. Effective confrontation asks the question: What can I do to help you succeed in living up to your values? In this case Paul is willing to cover all of the debt that Onesimus owes Philemon

Fifth, Paul builds accountability into the confrontation. He establishes that he will be visiting soon to see how things are going. Philemon knows that the Paul who cares about him will be checking in to see how he has responded to his confrontation. Part of accountability is the willingness to be visited with our progress. Friends who care enough to confront you with you own values are marvellous friends to have. Friends who follow up and care enough to hold you accountable for your growth are wonderful gifts from God.

It is not hard to see the Christ motif in Paul's approach. Two persons are to be reconciled in Paul, who bears the cost of that reconciliation personally. Following Paul's model, caring confrontation requires five things: a caring relationship; identification with the conflict of the other person; acceptance of a person's stated values and commitments as the starting point; a personal investment in the resolution; and a commitment to long term accountability and growth.

Conflict is inevitable in a Christian community. Yet conflict can be resolved through caring confrontation that invests itself in the growth and development of the other person.

But what about gossip? Why did I attach that item to a talk about confrontation and criticism? Because I believe that gossip has become the "pious" way to avoid confrontation and engage "nicely" in criticism within the Christian community.

Whether it happens in conversation or prayer or the horrible, "Here's something you might want to pray about!", gossip is a form of criticism that denies the caring commitment and love required by community. Gossip reveals a person who has not resolved his or her conflict, who is not growing. It does nothing to build community or the other person. Gossip takes criticism and whitewashes it with caring concern.

By gossip, I mean any negative comment about another person to a third person without the permission of the person being discussed. One of the tragedies of contemporary Christian community is that we avoid conflict, are afraid of confrontation and routinely engage in destructive gossip under the guise of spirituality. Gossip is inappropriate behaviour in a Christian community, and I for one am prepared to be held accountable to this belief by anyone who genuinely cares about me and my growth.

What I yearn for at Regent College is a community of people who so care for one another that we take the time to get to know each other, to understand one another's convictions, beliefs and commitments — that we care enough to engage each other in accountability relationships in which we give one another permission to confront us lovingly and hold us accountable for our growth and development before God. I would like to see us be a community where criticism and gossip are rejected and we hold one another accountable to eliminate them from our conversations.

May God bless this college with people who have the courage to risk an investment in community, to engage in genuine caring relationships, to confront one another and to be held accountable to our own intentional growth in Christ.

Regent Retreat
September 22, 1991

21

Going Back

*H*ow would you feel? You finally got out of that job that was grinding you down? Perhaps you did leave with some uncomfortable circumstances, but you took the step! You left to find yourself, to figure out what you are going to do with this life.

Away from your home, far from the responsibility of that earlier situation, you have time to do some thinking. And what a time — perhaps life changing!

Under the tutelage of new mentors, you begin to put the pieces of your life together. In the context of a new community, you meet the resurrected Christ and begin to think through the implications of his claim upon your life.

A community like this away from the pressures and responsibilities of your normal life is a gift from God — a privilege to be enjoyed and cherished. It is an opportunity to grow and to be changed. You are a different person than when you entered this community and sat at the feet of your mentor.

But now you are being sent back. Back to your community, back perhaps to uncomfortable circumstances, to old responsibilities and liabilities. You go back a new person — at least a changed person. What does it feel like to leave the community that nurtured your new growth and development, to go back to the people you left behind? That's the position that Onesimus found himself in.

Last fall we looked at the drama of Philemon, Onesimus, Paul and the

Colossian Church from the perspective of Philemon (Chapter 19) and the church (Chapter 20). We looked then at Paul's letter to Philemon and heard Paul calling him to account — to live up to the truth that he taught about community and to apply it to Onesimus. We looked at the responsibilities of community faced by the Colossian Church as they embrace the conflict between Philemon and Onesimus. I want to look at this story again, but this time through the eyes of Onesimus.

Onesimus had left his life in Colosse where he had been a slave on the staff of Philemon, a well-known leader in the Colossian church. Illegally he had run off, betraying his relationship of trust and probably to finance his trip, he stole from his master before he went.

Somehow in his flight, he ended up with the apostle Paul. We do not know the circumstances — how they met — how Paul ended up converting Onesimus to become a follower of Christ. But we do know that a strong relationship developed between Onesimus and his new mentor. He stayed with Paul, learned from him, cared for him and was loved by Paul in return. A close bond was formed between the two.

But somewhere in his education, somewhere in the discipling process, Paul and Onesimus agreed that it was time for him to return to Colosse — to go back to his community, return to his position as a slave of Philemon, restore the broken relationships and learn to serve God and grow within that community.

Paul writes a letter to Philemon to pave the way for Onesimus' return, building strongly on his personal relationships with Philemon and Onesimus. He also writes a letter to the Colossian church to encourage them since they will be the context of Christian community in which the reconciliation of one of their elders and his newly converted runaway slave must take place.

Paul then gives both letters and Onesimus to his friend and colleague Tychicus and sends him off to Colosse to make this all work — to show that Christian faith can be integrated into the fabric of life and work and relationships — that Christian community can deal with conflict and forgiveness and new beginnings. Paul sends Tychicus to encourage Philemon, Onesimus and the Colossians to listen to and learn from each other as they work out how their common faith will lead them through their damaged relationships and pain.

Some of you may be feeling a bit like Onesimus right now as you prepare to leave this place and return to your community. Hopefully, you do not have to face criminal judgement for a theft or something, but you do leave a place where you have been nurtured, where you have, we trust, encountered God and grown in your walk with Christ. And you do return to a community that has not shared this experience, this growth with you. Perhaps Onesimus' situation can be instructive for us as we prepare for our own returns and transitions.

Three things strike me about Onesimus' return:

1. He is leaving his mentor behind.
2. He has a friend to encourage him.
3. He is going back to serve.

Leaving mentors behind

It must have been a painful experience for Onesimus to leave Paul and return to Colosse. Not only was he leaving the man who had introduced him to Jesus, he was leaving a friend and a community of encouragement. He was leaving a place where he had grown — a place where he was loved — a place that valued him and his contribution — a place where his personal spiritual pilgrimage was understood. Onesimus was leaving the safety of a community which had shared his experience and nurtured his growth to enter a marketplace that was predisposed to accept him with hostility. He was leaving the comfort and security of the known to risk the unknown future. Perhaps some of you feel a bit like Onesimus as this year draws to a close and you prepare to leave this community and return to your corner of the marketplace.

Leaving is always hard. Separation causes pain and must be grieved, whether it be the loss of Gunther Strottehotte as he moves into the presence of God or the leaving of friends as you move out from this community. But this is where the resurrection life of Christian community takes over. We celebrated the defeat of death in resurrection life on Easter and we will celebrate your new life of ministry at Convocation. Separation in Christian community is always a mixture of grief and celebration.

Not only is the act of separation difficult, but the task of finding your new role, your new life and work, can often bring a crisis of identity. When you are a student you know who you are. It is always good to be a student! But afterwards, who am I? I remember feeling distinctly lost and adrift when I finished my doctoral studies and had to become a real person. Being a student is much nicer. It has a pleasant rhythm to life and limited responsibilities. Now you have to earn a living and make a contribution with your life. Responsibility and accountability hover over you like rain clouds even as you seek to enter the marketplace and live for God. Some of you are returning to positions — some already know the new responsibilities you will assume after Regent — and some of you leave with the uncertainty of your next step. For all of you who are leaving the community this year, this will be a time of transition, a time of change and perhaps uncertainty. But while you do leave your faculty mentors behind, you go out in the power of the Spirit of God. You go out as ambassadors of the Kingdom, and it is your relationship with God in Christ that must provide the security and identity for your own personal humanness if you are going to live for God in this world.

Leaving is hard, but it is necessary. The analogy of the butterfly fits well, I think. You cannot fly until you leave the cocoon. This week a person shared with me what she called the two objectives of parenting: *to provide roots and wings*. I hope this has been your experience at Regent this past year. Leadership, teaching, mentoring and parenting share these common objectives. I hope we have assisted you in deepening your theological and spiritual roots, and I hope we have empowered you to fly as you leave this community and wing your way around this world.

The mentoring relationship — the faculty-student relationship is an investment. People have invested in you this past year. God has provided for your education and growth. We pray that you will take this investment and share it with others. If you have been mentored — mentor someone else. If you have learned — teach. If you have been loved — love. If you have experienced community — build community. If you have met God — share him. If you have been prayed for — pray for others. The list could go on. But the point I want to make is that Convocation marks a transition — a transition from being mentored to mentoring others.

I still look back at my years of graduate study as formative for my life — but I remember the five years following graduate school as the best years of my life — a time when I began to test some of what I had learned. You have been taught, mentored and prayed for. Now it is your turn to be a mentor to those that God sends across your path.

The tradition of the early Church frequently equates the Onesimus of our story with the later Bishop Onesimus of Ephesus. This cannot be proved. But if it is true, the runaway slave from Colosse learned well from his mentors and became one who was regarded as a senior mentor and teacher in the church. From a slave of Philemon mentored by Paul, Onesimus may have become the Bishop of Ephesus, mentoring the leaders of the Church.

You leave this community next month because God has something for you to do as his ambassador to the marketplaces of this world. If you have been taught, go out and teach others.

Taking friends with you

The second thing I think we can learn from the Onesimus story is the importance of friends. Paul did not send Onesimus back to Colosse alone. He sent him with a friend —Tychicus. Tychicus is the least know member of this Colossian drama. He is a friend and colleague of Paul who was with Onesimus during his conversion and growth. He knows Onesimus well and we can assume that he has become an important friend to the converted slave.

When Paul sends Onesimus back to Colosse, he surely sent him out in the power of God. But he also sends with him a friend to support and encourage him as he returns to his home. Tychicus is there to encourage Onesimus as he faces Philemon — to confront Onesimus if he falters in his fear — to pave the way for him with Philemon and the Colossian Church — to pray for him and give advice as needed.

Again, the story has parallels for us. Now, most of you will not be taking a new friend from this community with you physically as you return to your marketplace. Some of you came with a friend or spouse who shared your experience and now returns with you. And I know at least three weddings are planned for Convocation day or shortly after: Ron and Dorothy, Libbie and Rodger, Mary and Karl have already identified their Tychicus. But for the rest of you, there is no reason why you cannot maintain your friendships even as you scatter. In this age of technology, it is easy to "reach out and touch someone." Friendships you have made here this past year do not need to end because we go in different directions. Commit yourselves to stay in touch, to pray for one another, to call, to write, to e-mail, to fax, to give encouragement and to ask how it is going.

When I left California to move to Regent almost four years ago, I left a very close, supporting community from Fuller, my church and my mountain-eering group. Leslie from Fuller called me weekly for the first months to see how I was doing and still calls nearly monthly to provide and receive encouragement. A group of managers meets weekly and prays for me each week. They call periodically to see how I am doing. Don and Brent, my mountaineering partners, immediately set up a permanent mountaineering schedule and we still get together for three trips per year. We also call one another at least monthly to say hello.

Beverly and I have invested in these relationships and in new ones since moving to Vancouver — and we work to maintain them. We get and send postcards, letters, e-mail and phone calls from all around the world as our friends move but stay in touch. In the last two weeks only, we received telephone calls from Australia, Taiwan, Italy and a postcard from the Philippines as well as phone calls from Memphis, Los Angeles, Seattle and Minneapolis. In each case there was no business to be conducted — simply friends checking in to remind us they still loved us and prayed for us and wanted to see how we were doing — invaluable relationships!

You have made important friendships during your time in this community. Set up plans now for how you will keep in touch over the years. It will require intentional action on your part. Relationships are subject to entropy. They deteriorate if not kept up. If you have valued the friendship and encouragement of the people around you this year, set up some on-going relationships that will continue to provide support and encouragement as you return to your various communities. Begin now to identify your Tychicus.

Going back to serve

The third thing we can learn from Onesimus may be the most important. *You are going back to serve.*

In our familiar views of Bible stories, we look back at what God has accomplished in his grace and often forget the feelings or anxieties of the person. We hear about Onesimus the Bishop and assume that God is sending Onesimus back to Colosse to become a bishop. Maybe this is true but Onesimus does not know it! Paul is only asking Philemon to receive him as a brother and reinstate him as his slave. Onesimus is going back to serve. He does not go back a free man. He goes back as Philemon's servant. The very act of returning to Colosse was an acknowledgement of this status and a willingness to serve.

That's the whole purpose of your time at Regent College. You have achieved learning, perhaps a degree, but you return as servants. We send you out today, back to your community, to your vocation, to your church, to serve. Perhaps you will become bishop, or president, or pastor or parent. But God usually doesn't advise us of these plans in advance. He sends us out as his ambassadors to serve those around us. More education does not necessarily mean more status, recognition and power. It simply means that you have more for which to be accountable in the expression of your service. We are equipped and educated to go out and serve.

Serving is being faithful to your calling at the moment wherever you find yourself. Maybe Onesimus did become Bishop. But he didn't go back to Colosse to be Bishop and do something great for God. He returned to be a servant.

You go out into the marketplace as new persons, refreshed and shaped by your experience in this community. Our community has invested in empowering you for leadership in this world and now we send you out as servants. They are one and the same.

Herman Hesse, in his little novel, *The Journey to the East*, describes a quest to discover the high council of a secret order in the East. The main characters are seeking to meet the leader of this society and be introduced to the fundamental truth of life. Throughout their journey they are guided and assisted by a servant assigned to care for them, carry their luggage and ease their passage. At the end, they finally arrive at the grand throne room of the society and who should walk out in the robes of the Grand Leader but their servant.

We send you out as leaders to make a difference in the world — and as servants to invest in the lives of those around you. If God has allowed this community to minister to you, go back to your community and replicate what you have valued here. Create community. If it was difficult here, it will be harder out there. But if you have tasted community, you know that it is worth the effort. Continue your own learning and growth. Education does not stop with Convocation. Learning to walk with God is a life-long experience. Get other people involved in their own theological education. Not everyone can come to Regent College. But everyone should be increasing in their knowledge of God and their growth in the Spirit. Find new mentors who will walk along side of you and invest yourselves as mentors in those that God brings into your lives.

Onesimus returned to Colosse after a time of instruction and growth with Paul and his friends. He left his mentor behind and returned to Colosse with a friend to take up his position as a slave to Philemon and a servant to his new master, Jesus Christ.

May God empower you with his Spirit for this next transition in your life. As you leave this community, may you take with you friendships that will follow you the rest of your life, may you find new mentors and offer yourself as a mentor to others and may you find abundant opportunities to serve "not only when their eye is on you, and to win their favour, but with sincerity of heart and reverence for the Lord. Whatever you do, work at it with all your heart, as working for the Lord, not for human masters, since you know that you will receive an inheritance from the Lord as a reward. It is the Lord Christ you are serving" (Colossians 3:22-24).

Regent Chapel
April 21, 1992

22
Leadership and Power

*T*he word of the Lord came to me: "Son of man, prophesy against the shepherds of Israel; prophesy and say to them: 'This is what the Sovereign Lord says: Woe to the shepherds of Israel who only take care of themselves! Should not shepherds take care of the flock? You eat the curds, clothe yourselves with the wool and slaughter the choice animals, but you do not take care of the flock. You have not strengthened the weak or healed the sick or bound up the injured. You have not brought back the strays or searched for the lost. You have ruled them harshly and brutally. So they were scattered because there was no shepherd, and when they were scattered they became food for all the wild animals. My sheep wandered over all the mountains and on every high hill. They were scattered over the whole earth, and no one searched or looked for them.*

"'Therefore, you shepherds, hear the word of the Lord: As surely as I live, declares the Sovereign Lord, because my flock lacks a shepherd and so has been plundered and has become food for all the wild animals, and because my shepherds did not search for my flock but cared for themselves

rather than for my flock, therefore, O shepherds, hear the word of the Lord: This is what the Sovereign Lord says: I am against the shepherds and will hold them accountable for my flock. I will remove them from tending the flock so that the shepherds can no longer feed themselves. I will rescue my flock from their mouths, and it will no longer be food for them.'"

Ezekiel 34:1-10

These people are blemishes at your love feasts, eating with you without the slightest qualm — shepherds who feed only themselves. They are clouds without rain, blown along by the wind; autumn trees, without fruit and uprooted — twice dead. They are wild waves of the sea, foaming up their shame; wandering stars, for whom blackest darkness has been reserved forever.

Jude 12- 13

They were the leaders — the political rulers and spiritual leaders of a mighty nation, a country blessed by God. They led a nation whose armed forces were respected beyond their relative size on the international scene. This was a country founded on high religious principles: one nation, living under God. A blessed country with natural and native resources, strategically positioned for strong international trade. The power and resources of these leaders of state and religion — the human, natural and spiritual potential for leadership on the world's stage were great.

And yet they were deposed from their offices. The political leaders fell to internal coups or were defeated in war. The religious leaders were written off as irrelevant for the modern people — the form of their piety and skill of their rhetoric were applauded, but they made no difference in the lives and behaviours of those around them. Why?

One man stood up and told them why — a preacher named Ezekiel. After the nation of Judah was defeated by Babylon, Jerusalem, its capital, was destroyed, and the people exiled to other countries — Ezekiel, a prophet and priest, living under the authority of his God, addressed the political and religious leaders with a message from God — *"Woe to the Shepherds of Israel, who only take care of themselves."* The leaders of Israel, political and religious, had used their power — the positions and resources which God had given them and their country — they had used their power for their own benefit, their own gain. They had gotten fat off the flock, but they had not used their power and authority to feed the flock, to care for and nurture the people for whom they were responsible. In his critique of their misdirected leadership, Ezekiel gives us an outline of God's expectations for the use of power — the exercise of leadership.

Before we look at Ezekiel's outline, we should clarify again our definitions. Leadership is a relationship between two people in which one seeks to influence the vision, values or behaviours of the other. It is relationships that make a difference in the lives of others. Today I want to talk about power. Power is a neutral term that denotes the potential for leadership. It refers to the personal gifts and resources or positional authority as perceived by others that enables persons to lead — to influence the people around them. It is the use and abuse of power that Ezekiel is addressing. He gives us four principles, I believe, for the appropriate use of power.

Biblical leadership uses power for the benefit of the people. Effective leadership uses its power and authority to grow and nurture the people, not the leader. The purpose of leadership points to the people. Power is not hoarded by the leader to serve the leader. (34:2-3)

Biblical leadership is empowering of others. Effective leadership strengthens those who are weakest, who have the least power. It brings back those who have strayed from the mission and values of the flock — the community or organization. (34:4)

Biblical leadership is caring, encouraging and motivating. Effective leadership is not coercive and dictatorial, but emerges from a caring relationship in which people are encouraged and motivated. It draws people together as an interdependent community or team rather than driving them into isolation and despair. Using power and position in a way that drives people away from the leader is not leadership. (34:4-6)

All leaders will be called to account for their exercise of power. Effective leadership is accountable. As the history of Israel and Judah illustrates, God, who is the source of all power and authority, will hold each person accountable for his or her use of these gifts. Those who do not lead effectively will be removed. (34:10) This accountability is not directed only at those in positions of leadership. It includes any member of the community whose strength, gifts or resources gives them more power than another member. Anyone who uses their strength — their power — to get fat while others are weak, stands accountable to God, says the prophet Ezekiel (34:20-21).

Having laid down this challenge to the leaders of his country, Ezekiel offers them hope that God will be their shepherd, caring for them, nurturing them, encouraging them and empowering them to care for and nurture one another, under his leadership (34:23).

Jude's challenge to Christian leaders

However, six hundred years later, we find that nothing has changed. In his little letter to those who would be leaders in a Christian community in the middle East, Jude, the brother of our Lord, challenges them for exactly the same misuse of their power and position. Jude is addressing his community of believers, counselling them against the leadership of some false teachers within their ranks who are flaunting their power and seeking to promote themselves as the leaders of this Christian community.

In his scathing critique of their leadership, Jude draws on five graphic images of poor leadership, and in doing so, like Ezekiel, gives us five working principles for effective biblical leadership.

The first image: *"Shepherds who feed only themselves"* — a poignant picture of leaders who use their power for their own benefit. As we see in Ezekiel and elsewhere, the shepherd is a common image of leadership in the Bible, modelling the care and investment that the leader must make for the growth and nurture of the followers. Jude, however, confronts the false leaders in the community to which he writes for precisely the same error that Ezekiel attacked. They are using their power not for the growth of the community, but to draw people to themselves, to put themselves on the pedestal, above the rules and values of the community. Biblical leadership, on the other hand, uses its power for the growth of the person being led.

Jude's second image is just as potent. *"Clouds without rain, blown along by the wind."* Imagine the farmer in the hot desert countryside trying to scratch out a living in the harsh climate. As he looks to the sky, he sees a cloud heading his way. The promise of rain looms large on his horizon; there is hope for the growth of his crops. And yet the cloud passes by, blown on the wind, failing to deliver on its promise, offering nothing for the growth of the crops — another powerful image. Jude is accusing the false leaders of promising growth, holding out hope to their followers, but not delivering. They are too intent on following their own desires and pursuing their spiritual visions to empower those they claim to lead. Biblical leadership offers hope and delivers on its promise. Biblical leadership empowers people. It makes a difference.

The third image: *"Autumn trees without fruit, up rooted — twice dead"* — another image expecting results. The leadership of the false teachers did not produce growth. There was no fruit, no product to show for the leadership that was being exercised. And Jude is not surprised since the leadership of the non-leaders is not rooted in the love of God for his people. They are doubly useless — not grounded in a relationship empowered by God and therefore not producing any growth in their community. Biblical leadership makes a difference — it produces growth in the followers as well as the leader.

"Wild waves of the sea, foaming up their shame." The fourth picture in Jude's graphic description picks up the biblical image of power in the waves of the sea and leaves us with the feeling of unbounded power, power without purpose, leaving a trail of debris behind it. The self-appointed leaders in the community were using their influence to make a big splash, but they were going nowhere. They were not working for the mission or unity of the community, but were divisive and contentious, flaunting a lifestyle that denied the lordship of Christ. Biblical leadership, on the other hand, points people away from the leader to the mission of the community and empowers their individual contribution towards that mission.

And finally, *"Wandering stars, for whom blackest darkness has been reserved forever."* This final image offers another timely corrective to false leadership. It portrays the leader who, like a shooting star, streaks onto the scene with flash and excitement but eventually fades and disappears. Short term gains but no long term perseverance. Leadership that may offer a quick fix but does not nurture the long range health of the community. Biblical leadership sees the future in God's hand and uses its power to influence people for the long run.

Five powerful images of leadership. While critiquing the leadership of the false teachers who are seeking to influence the community, Jude has given us five timeless characteristics of Biblical leadership:

1. Biblical leadership uses its power for the growth of the person being led.
2. Biblical leadership offers hope and delivers on its promise.

3. Biblical leadership makes a difference — it produces growth in the followers as well as the leader.
4. Biblical leadership points people away from the leader to the mission of the community and empowers their individual contribution towards that mission.
5. Biblical leadership sees the future in God's hand and uses its power to influence people for the long run.

Today the problem still exists

Now we are in the twentieth century, 2500 years after Ezekiel called the leaders of his day to account, 1900 years after Jude confronted those who sought to influence his community of believers. Not much has changed.

This year I received a Christmas card published by Inter-Varsity. Its cover dramatically reads "History is crowded with men who would be gods," and contains the pictures of nine great political and religious leaders who used their power for their own benefit. History is filled with men and women who have used their power to solidify their own positions, to work for their own gain. Positioned in the center of this card was the face of Adolf Hitler — a shepherd of our century who viciously fed off his flock.

Dietrich Bonhoeffer's book, *No Rusty Swords*, includes the powerful radio speech he gave in 1933 when Hitler came to power. He accuses Hitler of taking the power of the people for himself instead of using his power to lead the people for their growth and development. Hilter sought to be the Leader — *Der Fuhrer* — rather than to exercise responsible leadership. We celebrate that Hitler was removed from power and do not seem to mind that Bonhoeffer participated in an attempt to assassinate Hilter at one point in his career.

And look at last year: 1989 was an historical year, and a bad one for shepherds who feed only themselves. Last year we watched as history was rewritten. We cheered or at least were inwardly relieved when dictators were deposed. We saw Honecker and Krenz toppled in East Germany, Grosz in Hungary, the leadership of Czechoslovakia, Zhivkov in Bulgaria, Ceauseacu in Rumania, Noriega in Panama. Men who had used their power to build their own empires were finally called to account. While we were saddened by the bloodshed that was often included, we were pleased to see these leaders removed from their positions of power.

But we cringed when Jim Bakker was sent to prison. The problem hasn't changed. The accusation remains the same. Shepherds who feed themselves at the expense of the flock are accountable to God. This time, however, it's getting too close!

Today the problem still exists. Political leaders, organizational leaders and religious leaders still are tempted to use the position and power they are given to serve themselves instead of the people for whom they are responsible. The problem is still there, but where are the prophets? Where is Ezekiel, Jude or Bonhoeffer?

Interestingly enough, some of these prophets are coming out of the secular world of management. I find stronger voices against "fat shepherds" coming out of the current generation of management and leadership researchers and consultants. Paul Hersey, Peter Drucker, Tom Peters, Max DePree and Warren Bennis are just a few of the recent authors who pick up Ezekiel's challenge.

Over Christmas I read Warren Bennis's book, *On Becoming a Leader*. If I didn't know better, I might think I was reading Jim Houston! You don't become an effective leader by seeking to become a leader, says Bennis. You don't become a leader by "doing" things. Leaders are persons who focus on "being." They are persons who live out of the character of who they are. They give expression to their inner selves. Leaders who seek to lead by doing something are trying to prove themselves, Bennis says. True leaders are leaders because they are true to themselves and express themselves out of the integrity of their character. If Ezekiel or Jude could rephrase Bennis' words, they would say that true leaders rest in the security of their relationship with God and live out of this security. Then Ezekiel and Jude would add along with the management writers: these leaders would use the power and positions they are given to reach out in caring and nurturing relationships with those for whom they are responsible, those around them, to empower them for their own life and work in this world.

So What?

What does this mean for you? The key question I would like to leave with you is the one implied by Ezekiel and Jude: What will you do with your power? Will you lead, empower others or will you use your power for your own benefit — to gain recognition and solidify your position and stature?

Some of you might ask "What power?! I'm only a student with tuition bills and housing costs keeping me in near poverty!"

Remember though that power is the potential for leadership. It is the strength, gifts and resources that other people see in you that gives you the opportunity to lead — to influence their beliefs, their values, their behaviours. Knowledge is power, information is power, personal integrity and confidence of vision are perceived as power. The security you have in your own relationship with God gives you a spiritual power that can impact the lives of those around you. The investment you are making in your education this year — the investment the faculty is making in your spiritual and theological maturity — will result in resources and strength out of which you can lead.

Will you be a leader of the people of God? Will you make a difference in the lives of those around you? Whether you end up in a formal position of leadership or simply engage others in relationships, you are being equipped to lead. You are being equipped with knowledge, with a maturing relationship with God in Christ, with an integrated world view that empowers you to make a difference in the world.

Your decision is what you will do with this power. Will you use your new education, your spiritual maturity, for your own benefit, to find yourself . . . or will you use your power for the growth and nurture of other people? Will you empower others? Will you be caring, encouraging and motivating? Will you acknowledge your accountability to God? Will you offer hope and deliver what you promise? Will you make a difference in this world?

Don is a graduate of Regent College and now the president of a significant corporation in the States. He struggles to integrate his faith and his work — to use his power for the benefit of others. Don's employees want to work there — he gives value to their work. Don's customers come back — he cares for them and it shows. What to his colleagues is a very successful business is for Don the arena in which every decision is an expression of his integrated Christian world view.

Regent College might be used as another example. We are a well-fed flock! In 20 short years this college has become an internationally recognized theological school with a highly acclaimed faculty, an impressively motivated student body, a new building and a growing reputation. Much of the credit for this goes to the way God used the first two shepherds — two men sitting in our midst today. God used Jim Houston's and Carl Armerding's gifts and abilities to bring a vision into reality. The Board of Governors gave Jim and Carl authority — power to lead. Both men poured their lives into this community — they fed and nurtured the flock, they delivered the vision, they produced results, and they are staying for the long run, continuing to use their gifts to lead — to influence the people God sends to this community. They led the flock as one of the flock and continue to do so. They are shepherds who feed the flock.

When I travel, I am often asked what its like to be president of a college in which both my predecessors are still part of the community. I point out that there are seven former presidents and principals of theological schools on the Regent-Carey faculty! This is one of the signs of the health of this community. Regent College is a community of shepherds who see themselves as a flock. Carl's return this term to give leadership in Old Testament Studies is one more example of shepherds investing in the flock — a leader continuing to use his power to empower the people.

What about you? God has given you gifts and abilities. You are increasing your knowledge and skills. This gives you the power to make a difference in the lives of the people around you. You are a shepherd. And the prophets are waiting to pass judgment. How will you use the power that God has entrusted to you?

Regent Chapel
January 30, 1990

Epilogue

*A*s I read these talks again, I was not surprised to find that the audience had shifted. Originally of course they were delivered to the students, faculty and staff of Regent College at the opening and closing chapels of the academic year. But in this reading, God was talking to me because I find myself at a similar crossing in my journey with God. After 12 years in the Regent community, I am being led by God to a new adventure. I too am grieving the separation from friends, from a wonderful community in which I have become accustomed to seeing God at work. I too am standing on the threshold of a new experience with God. The anticipation and expectation are palpable. It is hard to leave a place where you have been with God. But it is exciting to go to a place where God will be. And that is the journey of the Christian life — the walk of a lifetime with God.

www.ingramcontent.com/pod-product-compliance
Lightning Source LLC
Chambersburg PA
CBHW031255090426
42742CB00007B/459